A New Day

A Daily Dose of Jesus Sprinkles!

Shunda White

A New Day: A Daily Dose of Jesus Sprinkles

©Shunda White 2017

Liberation's Publishing LLC ~ West Point, MS

Scripture quotations marked (KJV) matches the 1987 printing. The KJV is in the public domain in the United States.

Scripture quotations marked (AMP) are taken from the Amplified Bible, Copyright © 1954, 1958, 1962, 1964, 1965, 1987 by The Lockman Foundation. Used by permission.

ISBN-13: 978-1-7320846-5-0

January

Shunda White

A New Day: A Daily Dose of Jesus Sprinkles

January 1

Proverbs 3:9

"Honor the Lord with thy substance and with the first fruits of all thine increase

~KJV~

Honor the Lord with your wealth and the first fruits of all your crops (income);

~AMP~

January 2

Proverbs 3:10

So shall thy barns be filled with plenty and thy presses shall burst out with new wine.

~KJV~

Then your barns will be abundantly filled and your vats will overflow with new wine.

~AMP~

January 3

Luke 6:38

Give, and it shall be given unto you; good measure, pressed down, and shaken together, and running over, shall men give into your bosom. For with the same measure that ye mete withal it shall be measured to you again.

~KJV~

Give, and it will be given to you. They will pour into your lap a good measure—pressed down, shaken together, and running over [with no space left for more]. For with the standard of measurement you use [when you do good to others], it will be measured to you in return.

~AMP~

A New Day: *A Daily Dose of Jesus Sprinkles*

January 4

Matthew 10:8

Heal the sick, cleanse the lepers, arise the dead, cast out devils: freely ye have received, freely give.

~KJV~

"Heal the sick, raise the dead, cleanse the lepers, cast out demons. Freely you have received, freely give."

~AMP~

January 5

Acts 6:4

But we will give ourselves continually to prayer, and to the ministry of the word.

~KJV~

But we will [continue to] devote ourselves [steadfastly] to prayer and to the ministry of the word."

~AMP~

January 6

2 Corinthians 9:6 But this I say

He which soweth sparingly shall reap also sparingly; and he which soweth bountifully shall reap also bountifully.

~KJV~

Now [remember this: he who sows sparingly will also reap sparingly, and he who sows generously [that blessings may come to others] will also reap generously [and be blessed].

~AMP~

January 7

2 Corinthians 9:7

Every man according as he purposeth in his heart, so let him give; not grudgingly, or of necessity: for God loveth a cheerful giver.

~KJV~

Let each one give [thoughtfully and with purpose] just as he has decided in his heart, not grudgingly or under compulsion, for God loves a cheerful giver [and delights in the one whose heart is in his gift].

~AMP~

A New Day: A Daily Dose of Jesus Sprinkles

January 8

Proverbs 23:26

My son give me thine heart, and let thine eyes observe my ways.

~KJV~

My son, give me your heart
And let your eyes delight in my ways,
~AMP~

January 9

Psalm 109:4

For my love they are adversaries: but I give myself unto prayer.

~KJV~

In return for my love, they attack me,
But I am in prayer.

~AMP~

January 10

Exodus 30:15

The rich shall not give more, and the poor shall not give less than half a shekel, when they give an offering unto the Lord, to make an atonement for your souls.

~KJV~

The rich shall not give more, and the poor shall not give less than half a shekel, when they give an offering unto the Lord, to make an atonement for your souls.

~AMP~

January 11

Acts 20:35

I have showed up you all things, how that so laboring ye ought to support the weak and to remember the words of the Lord Jesus, how he said, "It is more blessed to give than to receive.

~KJV~

In everything I showed you [by example] that by working hard in this way you must help the weak and remember the words of the Lord Jesus, that He Himself said, 'It is more blessed [and brings greater joy] to give than to receive.'"

~AMP~

January 12

2 Peter 1:5

And Besides this, giving all diligence add to your faith virtue, and to virtue knowledge.

~KJV~

For this very reason, applying your diligence [to the divine promises, make every effort] in [exercising] your faith to, [a]develop moral excellence, and in moral excellence, knowledge (insight, understanding),

~AMP~

January 13

1 Timothy 4:13

Till I come, give attendance to reading, to exhortation, to doctrine.

~KJV~

Until I come, devote yourself to public reading [of Scripture], to preaching and to teaching [the sound doctrine of God's word].

~AMP~

January 14

Romans 13:7

Render Therefore to all their dues: tribute to whom tribute is due; custom to whom custom; feat to whom fear; honour to whom honour

~KJV~

Pay to all what is due: tax to whom tax is due, customs to whom customs, respect to whom respect, honor to whom honor.

~AMP~

January 15

1 Timothy 4:15

Meditate upon these things; give thyself wholly to them; that thy profiting may appear to all.

~KJV~

Practice and work hard on these things; be absorbed in them [completely occupied in your ministry], so that your progress will be evident to all.

~AMP~

January 16

Deuteronomy 26:2

That thou shalt take of the first of all the fruit of the earth, which thou shalt bring of thy land that the Lord thy God giveth thee, and shalt put it in a basket and shalt go unto the place which the Lord thy God shall choose to place his name there.

~KJV~

That you shall take some of the first of all the produce of the ground which you harvest from the land that the Lord your God gives you, and you shall put it in a basket and go to the [a]place where the Lord your God chooses to establish His Name (Presence).

~AMP~

January 17

Deuteronomy 16:17

Every man shall give as he is able according to the blessing of the Lord thy God which he hath given thee.

~KJV~

Every man shall give as he is able, in accordance with the blessing which the Lord your God has given you.

~AMP~

January 18

Matthew 7:11

If ye then, being evil know how to give good gifts unto your children, how much more shall your Father which is in heaven give good things to them that ask him.

~KJV~

If you then, evil (sinful by nature) as you are, know how to give good and advantageous gifts to your children, how much more will your Father who is in heaven [perfect as He is] give what is good and advantageous to those who keep on asking Him.

~AMP~

January 19

Genesis 28:22

And this stone, which I have set for a pillar, shall be God's house: and of all that thou shalt give me I will surely give the tenth unto thee.

~KJV~

This stone which I have set up as a pillar (monument, memorial) will be God's house [a sacred place to me], and of everything that You give me I will give the tenth to You [as an offering to signify my gratitude and dependence on You]."

~AMP~

January 20

Ecclesiastes 11:1

Cast thy bread upon the waters: for thou shalt find it after many days.

~KJV~

Cast your bread on the surface of the waters, [be diligently active, make thoughtful decisions], for you will find it after many days.

~AMP~

January 21

Ecclesiastes 11:2

Give a portion to seven, and also to eight; for thou knowest not what evil shall be upon the earth.

~KJV~

Give a portion to seven, or even [divide it] to eight, for you do not know what misfortune may occur on the earth.

~AMP~

January 22

Proverbs 19:17

He that hath pity upon the poor lendeth unto the Lord; and that which he hath given will he pay him again.

~KJV~

He who is gracious and lends a hand to the poor lends to the Lord, And the Lord will repay him for his good deed.

~AMP~

January 21

Ecclesiastes 11:2

Give a portion to seven, and also to eight; for thou knowest not what evil shall be upon the earth.

~KJV~

Give a portion to seven, or even [divide it] to eight, for you do not know what misfortune may occur on the earth.

~AMP~

January 22

Proverbs 19:17

He that hath pity upon the poor lendeth unto the Lord; and that which he hath given will he pay him again.

~KJV~

He who is gracious and lends a hand to the poor lends to the Lord, And the Lord will repay him for his good deed.

~AMP~

January 23

Hebrews 13:17

Obey them that have the rule over you, and submit yourselves: for they watch for your souls, as they that must give account, that they may do it with joy, and not with grief: for that is unprofitable for you.

~KJV~

Obey your [spiritual] leaders and submit to them [recognizing their authority over you], for they are keeping watch over your souls and continually guarding your spiritual welfare as those who will give an account [of their stewardship of you]. Let them do this with joy and not with grief and groans, for this would be of no benefit to you.

~AMP~

January 24

Matthew 6:1

Take heed that ye do not your alms before men, to be seen of them: otherwise ye have no reward of your Father which is in heaven.

~KJV~

"Be [very] careful not to do your good deeds publicly, to be seen by men; otherwise you will have no reward [prepared and awaiting you] with your Father who is in heaven.

~AMP~

January 25

Hosea 10:12

Sow to yourselves in righteousness, reap in mercy; break up your fallow ground: for it is time to seek the Lord, till he come and rain righteousness upon you.

~KJV~

Sow with a view to righteousness [that righteousness, like seed, may germinate]; Reap in accordance with mercy and lovingkindness. Break up your uncultivated ground, For it is time to seek and search diligently for the Lord [and to long for His blessing] Until He comes to rain righteousness and His gift of salvation on you.

~AMP~

January 26

Matthew 5:42

Give to him that asketh thee, and from him that would borrow of thee turn not thou away.

~KJV~

Give to him who asks of you, and do not turn away from him who wants to borrow from you.

~AMP~

January 27

Proverbs 3:27

Withhold not good from them to whom it is due, when it is in the power of thine hand to do it.

~KJV~

[a]Do not withhold good from those to whom it is due [its rightful recipients], When it is in your power to do it.

~AMP~

January 28

1 King 17:14

For thus saith the Lord God of Israel, The barrel of meal shall not waste, neither shall the cruse of oil fail, until the day that the Lord sendeth rain upon the earth.

~KJV~

For this is what the Lord God of Israel says: 'The bowl of flour shall not be exhausted nor shall the jar of oil be empty until the day that the Lord sends rain [again] on the face of the earth.'"

~AMP~

January 29

James 3:18

And the fruit of righteousness is sown in peace of them that make peace.

~KJV~

And the seed whose fruit is righteousness (spiritual maturity) is sown in peace by those who make peace [by actively encouraging goodwill between individuals].

~AMP~

January 30

Matthew 17:11

And Jesus answered and said unto them, Elias truly shall first come, and restore all things.

~KJV~

He answered and said, "Elijah is coming and will restore all things;

~AMP~

January 31

Malachi 3:10

Bring ye all the tithes into the storehouse, that there may be meat in mine house, and prove me now herewith, saith the Lord of hosts, if I will not open you the windows of heaven, and pour you out a blessing, that there shall not be room enough to receive it.

~KJV~

Bring all the tithes (the tenth) into the storehouse, so that there may be food in My house, and test Me now in this," says the Lord of hosts, "if I will not open for you the windows of heaven and pour out for you [so great] a blessing until there is no more room to receive it.

~AMP~

A New Day: A Daily Dose of Jesus Sprinkles

February

Shunda White

A New Day: A Daily Dose of Jesus Sprinkles

February 1

John 3:16

For God so loved the world, that he gave his only begotten Son, that whosoever believeth in him should not perish, but have everlasting life.

~KJV~

"For God so [greatly] loved and dearly prized the world, that He [even] gave His [One and] only begotten Son, so that whoever believes and trusts in Him [as Savior] shall not perish but have eternal life."

~AMP~

February 2

Leviticus 19:18

Thou shalt not avenge, nor bear any grudge against the children of thy people, but thou shalt love thy neighbour as thyself: I am the Lord.

~KJV~

You shall not take revenge nor bear any grudge against the sons of your people, but you shall love your neighbor (acquaintance, associate, companion) as yourself; I am the Lord.

~AMP~

February 3

Deuteronomy 6:5

And thou shalt love the Lord thy God with all thine heart, and with all thy soul, and with all thy might.

~KJV~

You shall love the Lord your God with all your heart and mind and with all your soul and with all your strength [your entire being].

~AMP~

February 4

John 13:34

A new commandment I give unto you, That ye love one another; as I have loved you, that ye also love one another.

~KJV~

I am giving you a new commandment, that you [a]love one another. Just as I have loved you, so you too are to love one another.

~AMP~

February 5

Amos 5:15

Hate the evil, and love the good, and establish judgment in the gate: it may be that the Lord God of hosts will be gracious unto the remnant of Joseph.

~KJV~

Hate evil and love good And establish justice in the [court of the city] gate. Perhaps the Lord God of hosts Will be gracious to the remnant of Joseph [that is, those who remain after God's judgment].

~AMP~

February 6

Galatians 5:22

But the fruit of the Spirit is love, joy, peace, longsuffering, gentleness, goodness, faith,

~KJV~

But the fruit of the Spirit [the result of His presence within us] is love [unselfish concern for others], joy, [inner] peace, patience [not the ability to wait, but how we act while waiting], kindness, goodness, faithfulness,

~AMP~

February 7

1 Timothy 1:5

Now the end of the commandment is charity out of a pure heart, and of a good conscience, and of faith unfeigned:

~KJV~

But the goal of our instruction is love [which springs] from a pure heart and a good conscience and a sincere faith.

~AMP~

February 8

Romans 13:8

Owe no man anything, but to love one another: for he that loveth another hath fulfilled the law.

~KJV~

[a]Owe nothing to anyone except to love and seek the best for one another; for he who [unselfishly] loves his neighbor has fulfilled the [essence of the] law [relating to one's fellowman].

~AMP~

February 9

Psalm 25:6

Remember, O Lord, thy tender mercies and thy lovingkindnesses; for they have been ever of old.

~KJV~

Remember, O Lord, Your [tender] compassion and Your loving kindnesses, For they have been from of old.

~AMP~

February 10

Romans 15:10

And again he saith, Rejoice, ye Gentiles, with his people.

~KJV~

Again it says, "Rejoice and celebrate, O Gentiles, along with His people."

~AMP~

February 11

Luke 7:47

Wherefore I say unto thee, Her sins, which are many, are forgiven; for she loved much: but to whom little is forgiven, the same loveth little.

~KJV~

Therefore I say to you, her sins, which are many, are forgiven, for she loved much; but he who is forgiven little, loves little."

~AMP~

February 12

John 15:12

This is my commandment, That ye love one another, as I have loved you.

~KJV~

"This is My commandment, that you love and unselfishly seek the best for one another, just as I have loved you.

~AMP~

February 13

Proverb 20:13

Love not sleep, lest thou come to poverty; open thine eyes, and thou shalt be satisfied with bread.

~KJV~

Do not love [excessive] sleep, or you will become poor; Open your eyes [so that you can do your work] and you will be satisfied with bread.

~AMP~

February 14

John 15:13

Greater love hath no man than this, that a man lay down his life for his friends.

~KJV~

No one has greater love [nor stronger commitment] than to lay down his own life for his friends.

~AMP~

February 15

John 15:17

These things I command you, that ye love one another.

~KJV~

This [is what] I command you: that you love and unselfishly seek the best for one another.

~AMP~

February 16

Ephesians 3:17

That Christ may dwell in your hearts by faith; that ye, being rooted and grounded in love,

~KJV~

so that Christ may dwell in your hearts through your faith. And may you, having been [deeply] rooted and [securely] grounded in love,

~AMP~

February 17

Proverbs 17:17

A friend loveth at all times, and a brother is born for adversity.

~KJV~

A friend loves at all times,
And a brother is born for adversity.

~AMP~

February 18

Romans 12:9

Let love be without dissimulation. Abhor that which is evil; cleave to that which is good.

~KJV~

Love is to be sincere and active [the real thing—without guile and hypocrisy]. Hate what is evil [detest all ungodliness, do not tolerate wickedness]; hold on tightly to what is good.

~AMP~

February 19

Romans 12:10

Be kindly affectioned one to another with brotherly love; in honour preferring one another;

~KJV~

Be devoted to one another with [authentic] brotherly affection [as members of one family], give preference to one another in honor;

~AMP~

February 20

1 John 2:15

Love not the world, neither the things that are in the world. If any man love the world, the love of the Father is not in him.

~KJV~

Do not love the world [of sin that opposes God and His precepts], nor the things that are in the world. If anyone loves the world, the love of the Father is not in him.

~AMP~

February 21

Ephesians 4:2

With all lowliness and meekness, with longsuffering, forbearing one another in love;

~KJV~

With all humility [forsaking self-righteousness], and gentleness [maintaining self-control], with patience, bearing with one another in [unselfish] love.

~AMP~

A New Day: *A Daily Dose of Jesus Sprinkles*

February 22

Hebrews 13:1

Let brotherly love continue.

~KJV~

Let love of your fellow believers continue.

~AMP~

February 23

1 Corinthians 13:1

Though I speak with the tongues of men and of angels, and have not charity, I am become as sounding brass, or a tinkling cymbal.

~KJV~

If I speak with the tongues of men and of angels, but have not love [for others growing out of God's love for me], then I have become only a noisy gong or a clanging cymbal [just an annoying distraction].

~AMP~

February 24

1 Corinthians 13:2

And though I have the gift of prophecy, and understand all mysteries, and all knowledge; and though I have all faith, so that I could remove mountains, and have not charity, I am nothing.

~KJV~

And if I have the gift of prophecy [and speak a new message from God to the people], and understand all mysteries, and [possess] all knowledge; and if I have all [sufficient] faith so that I can remove mountains, but do not have love [reaching out to others], I am nothing.

~AMP~

February 25

1 Corinthians 13:3

And though I bestow all my goods to feed the poor, and though I give my body to be burned, and have not charity, it profiteth me nothing.

~KJV~

If I give all my possessions to feed the poor, and if I surrender my body to be burned, but do not have love, it does me no good at all.

~AMP~

A New Day: A Daily Dose of Jesus Sprinkles

February 26
1 Corinthians 13:4-7

Charity suffereth long and is kind; charity envieth not; charity vaunteth not itself, is not puffed up, 5 Doth not behave itself unseemly, seeketh not her own, is not easily provoked, thinketh no evil; 6 Rejoiceth not in iniquity, but rejoiceth in the truth; 7 Beareth all things, believeth all things, hopeth all things, endureth all things.

~KJV~

4 Love endures with patience and serenity, love is kind and thoughtful, and is not jealous or envious; love does not brag and is not proud or arrogant. 5 It is not rude; it is not self-seeking, it is not provoked [nor overly sensitive and easily angered]; it does not take into account a wrong endured. 6 It does not rejoice at injustice but rejoices with the truth [when right and truth prevail]. 7 Love bears all things [regardless of what comes], believes all things [looking for the best in each one], hopes all things [remaining steadfast during difficult times], endures all things [without weakening].

~AMP~

February 27

1 Corinthians 13:8

Charity never faileth: but whether there be prophecies, they shall fail; whether there be tongues, they shall cease; whether there be knowledge, it shall vanish away.

~KJV~

Love never fails [it never fades nor ends]. But as for prophecies, they will pass away; as for tongues, they will cease; as for the gift of special knowledge, it will pass away.

~AMP~

February 28

1 Corinthians 13:13

And now abideth faith, hope, charity, these three; but the greatest of these is charity.

~KJV~

And now there remain: faith [abiding trust in God and His promises], hope [confident expectation of eternal salvation], love [unselfish love for others growing out of God's love for me], these three [the choicest graces]; but the greatest of these is love.

~AMP~

February 29

Revelations 3:19

As many as I love, I rebuke and chasten: be zealous therefore, and repent.

~KJV~

Those whom I [dearly and tenderly] love, I rebuke and discipline [showing them their faults and instructing them]; so be enthusiastic and repent [change your inner self—your old way of thinking, your sinful behavior—seek God's will].

~AMP~

A New Day: A Daily Dose of Jesus Sprinkles

March

Shunda White

A New Day: A Daily Dose of Jesus Sprinkles

March 1

Hebrews 13:2

Be not forgetful to entertain strangers: for thereby some have entertained angels unawares.

~KJV~

Do not neglect to extend hospitality to strangers [especially among the family of believers—being friendly, cordial, and gracious, sharing the comforts of your home and doing your part generously], for by this some have entertained angels without knowing it.

~AMP~

March 2

Isaiah 55:6

Seek ye the Lord while he may be found, call ye upon him while he is near:

~KJV~

Seek the Lord while He may be found;
Call on Him [for salvation] while He is near.
~AMP~

March 3

Isaiah 1:18

Come now, and let us reason together, saith the Lord: though your sins be as scarlet, they shall be as white as snow; though they be red like crimson, they shall be as wool.

~KJV~

"Come now, and let us reason together," Says the Lord. "Though your sins are like scarlet, They shall be as white as snow; Though they are red like crimson, They shall be like wool.

~AMP~

March 4

Proverbs 22:4

By humility and the fear of the Lord are riches, and honour, and life.

~KJV~

The reward of humility [that is, having a realistic view of one's importance] and the [reverent, worshipful] fear of the Lord Is riches, honor, and life.

~AMP~

March 5
Proverbs 30:5

Every word of God is pure: he is a shield unto them that put their trust in him.
~KJV~

Every word of God is tested and refined [like silver]; He is a shield to those who trust and take refuge in Him.
~AMP~

March 6
Proverbs 3:5

Trust in the Lord with all thine heart; and lean not unto thine own understanding.
~KJV~

Trust in and rely confidently on the Lord with all your heart and do not rely on your own insight or understanding.
~AMP~

March 7

Proverbs 3:6

In all thy ways acknowledge him, and he shall direct thy paths.

~KJV~

In all your ways know and acknowledge and recognize Him, And He will make your paths straight and smooth [removing obstacles that block your way].

~AMP~

March 8

Proverbs 6:2

Thou art snared with the words of thy mouth, thou art taken with the words of thy mouth.

~KJV~

If you have been snared with the words of your lips, If you have been trapped by the speech of your mouth,

~AMP~

March 9

Isaiah 1:19

If ye be willing and obedient, ye shall eat the good of the land:

~KJV~

"If you are willing and obedient, You shall eat the best of the land;

~AMP~

March 10

Psalm 119:133

Order my steps in thy word: and let not any iniquity have dominion over me.

~KJV~

Establish my footsteps in [the way of] Your word; Do not let any human weakness have power over me [causing me to be separated from You].

~AMP~

March 11

Psalm 119:103

How sweet are thy words unto my taste! yea, sweeter than honey to my mouth!

~KJV~

How sweet are Your words to my taste, Sweeter than honey to my mouth!

~AMP~

March 12

Psalm 119:105

Thy word is a lamp unto my feet, and a light unto my path.

~KJV~

Your word is a lamp to my feet And a light to my path.

~AMP~

March 13

Ephesians 6:13

Wherefore take unto you the whole armour of God, that ye may be able to withstand in the evil day, and having done all, to stand.

~KJV~

Therefore, put on the complete armor of God, so that you will be able to [successfully] resist and stand your ground in the evil day [of danger], and having done everything [that the crisis demands], to stand firm [in your place, fully prepared, immovable, victorious].

~AMP~

March 14

Ephesians 6:14

Stand therefore, having your loins girt about with truth, and having on the breastplate of righteousness;

~KJV~

So stand firm and hold your ground, having tightened the wide band of truth (personal integrity, moral courage) around your waist and having put on the breastplate of righteousness (an upright heart),

~AMP~

March 15

Ephesians 6:15

"And your feet shod with the preparation of the gospel of peace;"

~KJV~

"and having strapped on your feet the gospel of peace in preparation [to face the enemy with firm-footed stability and the readiness produced by the good news].

~AMP~

A New Day: A Daily Dose of Jesus Sprinkles

March 16

John 3:16

For God so loved the world, that he gave his only begotten Son, that whosoever believeth in him should not perish, but have everlasting life.

~KJV~

"For God so [greatly] loved and dearly prized the world, that He [even] gave His [One and] [a]only begotten Son, so that whoever believes and trusts in Him [as Savior] shall not perish, but have eternal life."

~AMP~

March 17

Isaiah 54:17

No weapon that is formed against thee shall prosper; and every tongue that shall rise against thee in judgment thou shalt condemn. This is the heritage of the servants of the Lord, and their righteousness is of me, saith the Lord.

~KJV~

"No weapon that is formed against you will succeed; And every tongue that rises against you in judgment you will condemn. This [peace, righteousness, security, and triumph over opposition] is the heritage of the servants of the Lord, And this is their vindication from Me," says the Lord.

~AMP~

March 18

Ephesians 6:18

Praying always with all prayer and supplication in the Spirit, and watching thereunto with all perseverance and supplication for all saints;

~KJV~

With all prayer and petition pray [with specific requests] at all times [on every occasion and in every season] in the Spirit, and with this in view, stay alert with all perseverance and petition [interceding in prayer] for all God's people.

~AMP~

March 19

Ephesians 5:17

Wherefore be ye not unwise, but understanding what the will of the Lord is.

~KJV~

Therefore do not be foolish and thoughtless, but understand and firmly grasp what the will of the Lord is.

~AMP~

March 20

Acts 1:8

But ye shall receive power, after that the Holy Ghost is come upon you: and ye shall be witnesses unto me both in Jerusalem, and in all Judaea, and in Samaria, and unto the uttermost part of the earth.

~KJV~

But you will receive power and ability when the Holy Spirit comes upon you; and you will be My witnesses [to tell people about Me] both in Jerusalem and in all Judea, and Samaria, and even to the ends of the earth."

~AMP~

March 21

Proverbs 1:23

Turn you at my reproof: behold, I will pour out my spirit unto you, I will make known my words unto you.

~KJV~

"If you will turn and pay attention to my rebuke, Behold, I [Wisdom] will pour out my spirit on you; I will make my words known to you.

~AMP~

March 22

Proverbs 22:1

A good name is rather to be chosen than great riches, and loving favour rather than silver and gold.

~KJV~

A good name [earned by honorable behavior, godly wisdom, moral courage, and personal integrity] is more desirable than great riches; And favor is better than silver and gold.

~AMP~

March 23

Psalm 23:1

The Lord is my shepherd; I shall not want.

~KJV~

The Lord is my Shepherd [to feed, to guide and to shield me], I shall not want.

~AMP~

March 24

Ephesians 6:16

Above all, taking the shield of faith, wherewith ye shall be able to quench all the fiery darts of the wicked.

~KJV~

Above all, lift up the [protective] shield of faith with which you can extinguish all the flaming arrows of the evil one.

~AMP~

March 25

Ephesians 6:17

And take the helmet of salvation, and the sword of the Spirit, which is the word of God:

~KJV~

And take the HELMET OF SALVATION, and the sword of the Spirit, which is the Word of God.

~AMP~

A New Day: *A Daily Dose of Jesus Sprinkles*

March 26

Isaiah 41:10

Fear thou not; for I am with thee: be not dismayed; for I am thy God: I will strengthen thee; yea, I will help thee; yea, I will uphold thee with the right hand of my righteousness.

~KJV~

'Do not fear [anything], for I am with you; Do not be afraid, for I am your God. I will strengthen you, be assured I will help you; I will certainly take hold of you with My righteous right hand [a hand of justice, of power, of victory, of salvation].'

~AMP~

March 27

Psalm 137:2

We hanged our harps upon the willows in the midst thereof.

~KJV~

On the willow trees in the midst of Babylon we hung our harps.

~AMP~

March 28

John 12:26

If any man serve me, let him follow me; and where I am, there shall also my servant be: if any man serve me, him will my Father honour.

~KJV~

If anyone serves Me, he must [continue to faithfully] follow Me [without hesitation, holding steadfastly to Me, conforming to My example in living and, if need be, suffering or perhaps dying because of faith in Me]; and wherever I am [in heaven's glory], there will My servant be also. If anyone serves Me, the Father will honor him.

~AMP~

March 29

Psalm 150:1

Praise ye the Lord. Praise God in his sanctuary: praise him in the firmament of his power.

~KJV~

Praise the Lord! Praise God in His sanctuary; Praise Him in His mighty heavens.

~AMP~

March 30

Psalm 150:2

Praise him for his mighty acts: praise him according to his excellent greatness.

~KJV~

Praise Him for His mighty acts; Praise Him according to [the abundance of] His greatness.

~AMP~

March 31

Psalm 150:6

Let everything that hath breath praise the Lord. Praise ye the Lord.

~KJV~

Let everything that has breath and every breath of life praise the Lord! Praise the Lord! (Hallelujah!)

~AMP~

A New Day: *A Daily Dose of Jesus Sprinkles*

April

Shunda White

A New Day: *A Daily Dose of Jesus Sprinkles*

April 1
Psalm 1:1

Blessed is the man that walketh not in the counsel of the ungodly, nor standeth in the way of sinners, nor sitteth in the seat of the scornful.
~KJV~

[a]Blessed [fortunate, prosperous, and favored by God] is the man who does not walk in the counsel of the wicked [following their advice and example],
Nor stand in the path of sinners,
Nor sit [down to rest] in the seat of scoffers (ridiculers).
~AMP~

April 2
Psalm 1:2

But his delight is in the law of the Lord; and in his law doth he meditate day and night.
~KJV~

But his delight is in the law of the Lord,
And on His law [His precepts and teachings] he [habitually] meditates day and night.
~AMP~

April 3
Psalm 1:3

And he shall be like a tree planted by the rivers of water, that bringeth forth his fruit in his season; his leaf also shall not wither; and whatsoever he doeth shall prosper.
~KJV~

And he will be like a tree firmly planted [and fed] by streams of water, Which yields its fruit in its season; Its leaf does not wither; And in whatever he does, he prospers [and comes to maturity].
~AMP~

April 4
John 8:32

And ye shall know the truth, and the truth shall make you free.
~KJV~

And you will know the truth [regarding salvation], and the truth will set you free [from the penalty of sin]."

~AMP~

April 5
John 15:5

I am the vine, ye are the branches: He that abideth in me, and I in him, the same bringeth forth much fruit: for without me ye can do nothing.

~KJV~

[a]I am the Vine; you are the branches. The one who remains in Me and I in him bears much fruit, for [otherwise] apart from Me [that is, cut off from vital union with Me] you can do nothing.

~AMP~

April 6

John 15:6

If a man abide not in me, he is cast forth as a branch, and is withered; and men gather them, and cast them into the fire, and they are burned.

~KJV~

If anyone does not remain in Me, he is thrown out like a [broken off] branch, and withers and dies; and they gather such branches and throw them into the fire, and they are burned.

~AMP~

April 7
John 15:7

If ye abide in me, and my words abide in you, ye shall ask what ye will, and it shall be done unto you.

~KJV~

If you remain in Me and My words remain in you [that is, if we are vitally united and My message lives in your heart], ask whatever you wish and it will be done for you.

~AMP~

April 8

John 3:3

Jesus answered and said unto him, Verily, verily, I say unto thee, Except a man be born again, he cannot see the kingdom of God.

~KJV~

Jesus answered him, "I assure you and most solemnly say to you, unless a person is born again [reborn from above—spiritually transformed, renewed, sanctified], he cannot [ever] see and experience the kingdom of God."

~AMP~

April 9
John 15:9

As the Father hath loved me, so have I loved you: continue ye in my love

~KJV~

I have loved you just as the Father has loved Me; remain in My love [and do not doubt My love for you].

~AMP~

April 10

John 15:10

If ye keep my commandments, ye shall abide in my love; even as I have kept my Father's commandments, and abide in his love.

~KJV~

If you keep My commandments and obey My teaching, you will remain in My love, just as I have kept My Father's commandments and remain in His love.

~AMP~

April 11

Psalm 33:8

Let all the earth fear the Lord: let all the inhabitants of the world stand in awe of him.

~KJV~

Let all the earth fear and worship the Lord; Let all the inhabitants of the world stand in awe of Him.

~AMP~

April 12

Psalm 33:12

Blessed is the nation whose God is the Lord; and the people whom he hath chosen for his own inheritance.

~KJV~

Blessed [fortunate, prosperous, and favored by God] is the nation whose God is the Lord, The people whom He has chosen as His own inheritance.

~AMP~

April 13

John 16:13

Howbeit when he, the Spirit of truth, is come, he will guide you into all truth: for he shall not speak of himself; but whatsoever he shall hear, that shall he speak: and he will shew you things to come.

~KJV~

But when He, the Spirit of Truth, comes, He will guide you into all the truth [full and complete truth]. For He will not speak on His own initiative, but He will speak whatever He hears [from the Father—the message regarding the Son], and He will disclose to you what is to come [in the future].

~AMP~

April 14

John 16:14

He shall glorify me: for he shall receive of mine, and shall shew it unto you.

~KJV~

He will glorify and honor Me, because He (the Holy Spirit) will take from what is Mine and will disclose it to you.

~AMP~

April 15

Romans 8:28

And we know that all things work together for good to them that love God, to them who are the called according to his purpose.

~KJV~

And we know [with great confidence] that God [who is deeply concerned about us] causes all things to work together [as a plan] for good for those who love God, to those who are called according to His plan and purpose.

~AMP~

April 16

John 3:16

For God so loved the world, that he gave his only begotten Son, that whosoever believeth in him should not perish, but have everlasting life.

~KJV~

"For God so [greatly] loved and dearly prized the world, that He [even] gave His [One and] only begotten Son, so that whoever believes and trusts in Him [as Savior] shall not perish, but have eternal life.

~AMP~

April 17

Romans 8:35

Who shall separate us from the love of Christ? shall tribulation, or distress, or persecution, or famine, or nakedness, or peril, or sword?

~KJV~

Who shall ever separate us from the love of Christ? Will tribulation, or distress, or persecution, or famine, or nakedness, or danger, or sword?

~AMP~

April 18
Joshua 1:8

This book of the law shall not depart out of thy mouth; but thou shalt meditate therein day and night, that thou mayest observe to do according to all that is written therein: for then thou shalt make thy way prosperous, and then thou shalt have good success.

~KJV~

This Book of the Law shall not depart from your mouth, but you shall read [and meditate on] it day and night, so that you may be careful to do [everything] in accordance with all that is written in it; for then you will make your way prosperous, and then you will be [a]successful.

~AMP~

April 19

1 Corinthians 9:24

Know ye not that they which run in a race run all, but one receiveth the prize? So run, that ye may obtain.

~KJV~

[a]Do you not know that in a race all the runners run [their very best to win], but only one receives the prize? Run [your race] in such a way that you may seize the prize and make it yours!

~AMP~

April 20

Matthew 6:6

But thou, when thou prayest, enter into thy closet, and when thou hast shut thy door, pray to thy Father which is in secret; and thy Father which seeth in secret shall reward thee openly.

~KJV~

But when you pray, go into your most private room, close the door and pray to your Father who is in secret, and your Father who sees [what is done] in secret will reward you.

~AMP~

April 21

Matthew 6:8

Be not ye therefore like unto them: for your Father knoweth what things ye have need of, before ye ask him.

~KJV~

So do not be like them [praying as they do]; for your Father knows what you need before you ask Him.

~AMP~

April 22

Matthew 6:24

No man can serve two masters: for either he will hate the one, and love the other; or else he will hold to the one, and despise the other. Ye cannot serve God and mammon.

~KJV~

"No one can serve two masters; for either he will hate the one and love the other, or he will be devoted to the one and despise the other. You cannot serve God and mammon [money, possessions, fame, status, or whatever is valued more than the Lord].

~AMP~

April 23

1 Corinthians 12:31

But covet earnestly the best gifts: and yet shew I unto you a more excellent way.

~KJV~

But earnestly desire and strive for the greater gifts [if acquiring them is going to be your goal]. And yet I will show you a still more excellent way [one of the choicest graces and the highest of them all: unselfish love].

~AMP~

April 24

John 16:24

Hitherto have ye asked nothing in my name: ask, and ye shall receive, that your joy may be full.

~KJV~

Until now you have not asked [the Father] for anything in My name; but now ask and keep on asking and you will receive, so that your joy may be full and complete.

~AMP~

April 25

1 Corinthians 14:33

For God is not the author of confusion, but of peace, as in all churches of the saints.

~KJV~

for God [who is the source of their prophesying] is not a God of confusion and disorder but of peace and order. As [is the practice] in all the churches of the saints (God's people),

~AMP~

April 26

Psalm 46:9

He maketh wars to cease unto the end of the earth; he breaketh the bow, and cutteth the spear in sunder; he burneth the chariot in the fire.

~KJV~

He makes wars to cease to the end of the earth; He breaks the bow into pieces and snaps the spear in two; He burns the chariots with fire.

~AMP~

April 27

Psalm 47:9

The princes of the people are gathered together, even the people of the God of Abraham: for the shields of the earth belong unto God: he is greatly exalted.

~KJV~

The princes of the people have gathered together as the people of the God of Abraham, For the shields of the earth belong to God; He is highly exalted.

~AMP~

April 28

Jude 24

Now unto him that is able to keep you from falling, and to present you faultless before the presence of his glory with exceeding joy,

~KJV~

Now to Him who is able to keep you from stumbling or falling into sin, and to present you unblemished [blameless and faultless] in the presence of His glory with triumphant joy and unspeakable delight,

~AMP~

April 29

Jude 25

To the only wise God our Saviour, be glory and majesty, dominion and power, both now and ever. Amen.

~KJV~

to the only God our Savior, through Jesus Christ our Lord, be glory, majesty, dominion, and power, before all time and now and forever. Amen.

~AMP~

April 30

Matthew 6:33

But seek ye first the kingdom of God, and his righteousness; and all these things shall be added unto you.

~KJV~

But first and most importantly seek (aim at, strive after) His kingdom and His righteousness [His way of doing and being right—the attitude and character of God], and all these things will be given to you also.

~AMP~

Shunda White

May

A New Day: *A Daily Dose of Jesus Sprinkles*

May 1

Genesis 3:20

And Adam called his wife's name Eve; because she was the mother of all living.

~KJV~

The man named his wife Eve (life spring, life giver), because she was the mother of all the living.

~AMP~

May 2

Genesis 17:16

And I will bless her, and give thee a son also of her: yea, I will bless her, and she shall be a mother of nations; kings of people shall be of her.

~KJV~

I will bless her, and indeed I will also give you a son by her. Yes, I will bless her, and she shall be a mother of nations; kings of peoples will come from her."

~AMP~

May 3

Exodus 20:12

Honour thy father and thy mother: that thy days may be long upon the land which the Lord thy God giveth thee.

~KJV~

"Honor (respect, obey, care for) your father and your mother, so that your days may be prolonged in the land the Lord your God gives you.

~AMP~

May 4

Matthew 15:4

For God commanded, saying, Honour thy father and mother: and, He that curseth father or mother, let him die the death.

~KJV~

For God said [through Moses], 'HONOUR YOUR FATHER AND MOTHER," AND 'HE WHO SPEAKS EVIL OF OR INSULT OR TREATS MPROPERLY FATHER OR MOTHER IS TO BE PUT TO DEATH.'

~AMP~

May 5

Mark 10:19

Thou knowest the commandments, Do not commit adultery, Do not kill, Do not steal, Do not bear false witness, Defraud not, Honour thy father and mother.

~KJV~

You know the commandments: DO NOT MURDER, DO NOT COMMIT ADULTERY, DO NOT STEAL, DO NOT TESTIFY FALSELY, DO NOT DEFRAUD, HONOR YOUR FATHER AND MOTHER"

~AMP~

May 6

John 3:3

Jesus answered and said unto him, Verily, verily, I say unto thee, Except a man be born again, he cannot see the kingdom of God.

~KJV~

Jesus answered him, "I assure you and most solemnly say to you, unless a person is born again [reborn from above—spiritually transformed, renewed, sanctified], he cannot [ever] see and experience the kingdom of God."

~AMP~

May 7

John 3:4

Nicodemus saith unto him, How can a man be born when he is old? can he enter the second time into his mother's womb, and be born?

~KJV~

Nicodemus said to Him, "How can a man be born when he is old? He cannot enter his mother's womb a second time and be born, can he?"

~AMP~

May 8

John 3:5

Jesus answered, Verily, verily, I say unto thee, Except a man be born of water and of the Spirit, he cannot enter into the kingdom of God.

~KJV~

Jesus answered, "I assure you and most solemnly say to you, unless one is born of water and the Spirit he cannot [ever] enter the kingdom of God.

~AMP~

May 9

Psalms 22:9

But thou art he that took me out of the womb: thou didst make me hope when I was upon my mother's breasts.

~KJV~

Yet You are He who pulled me out of the womb; You made me trust when on my mother's breasts.

~AMP~

May 10

Mark 7:10

For Moses said, Honour thy father and thy mother; and, Whoso curseth father or mother, let him die the death:

~KJV~

For Moses said, 'HONOR YOUR FATHER AND YOUR MOTHER [WITH RESPECT AND GRATITUDE] AND, 'HE WHO SPEAKS EVIL OF HIS FATHER OR MOTHER MUST BE PUT TO DEATH;

~AMP~

May 11

Mark 7:11

But ye say, If a man shall say to his father or mother, It is Corban, that is to say, a gift, by whatsoever thou mightest be profited by me; he shall be free.

~KJV~

but you [Pharisees and scribes] say, 'If a man tells his father or mother, "Whatever I have that would help you is Corban, (that is to say, already a gift to God),"'

~AMP~

May 12

Hebrews 7:3

Without father, without mother, without descent, having neither beginning of days, nor end of life; but made like unto the Son of God; abideth a priest continually.

~KJV~

Without [[a]any record of] father or mother, nor ancestral line, without [any record of] beginning of days (birth) nor ending of life (death), but having been made like the Son of God, he remains a priest without interruption and without successor.

~AMP~

May 13

Galatians 1:15

But when it pleased God, who separated me from my mother's womb, and called me by his grace,

~KJV~

But when God, who had chosen me and set me apart before I was born, and called me through His grace, was pleased

~AMP~

May 14

Galatians 1:16

To reveal his Son in me, that I might preach him among the heathen; immediately I conferred not with flesh and blood:

~KJV~

to reveal His Son in me so that I might preach Him among the Gentiles [as the good news—the way of salvation], I did not immediately consult with [a]anyone [for guidance regarding God's call and His revelation to me].

~AMP~

May 15

Luke 1:15

"For he shall be great in the sight of the Lord, and shall drink neither wine nor strong drink; and he shall be filled with the Holy Ghost, even from his mother's womb."

~KJV~

"for he will be great and distinguished in the sight of the Lord; and will never drink wine or liquor, and he will be filled with and empowered to act by the Holy Spirit while still in his mother's womb."

~AMP~

May 16

Deuteronomy 5:16

"Honour thy father and thy mother, as the Lord thy God hath commanded thee; that thy days may be prolonged, and that it may go well with thee, in the land which the Lord thy God giveth thee."

~KJV~

"Honor (respect, obey, care for) your father and your mother, as the Lord your God has commanded you, so that your days [on the earth] may be prolonged and so that it may go well with you in the land which the Lord your God gives you."

~AMP~

May 17

John 3:16

For God so loved the world, that he gave his only begotten Son, that whosoever believeth in him should not perish, but have everlasting life.

~KJV~

"For God so [greatly] loved and dearly prized the world, that He [even] gave His [One and] [a]only begotten Son, so that whoever believes and trusts in Him [as Savior] shall not perish, but have eternal life.

~AMP~

May 18

1 Samuel 1:13

Now Hannah, she spake in her heart; only her lips moved, but her voice was not heard: therefore Eli thought she had been drunken.

~KJV~

Hannah was speaking in her heart (mind); only her lips were moving, and her voice was not heard, so Eli thought she was drunk.

~AMP~

May 19

Matthew 19:19

Honour thy father and thy mother: and, Thou shalt love thy neighbour as thyself.

~KJV~

HONOR YOUR FATHER AND MOTHER; AND LOVE YOUR NEIGHBOR AS YOURSELF" [that is, unselfishly seek the best or higher good for others].

~AMP~

May 20

Romans 16:3

Greet Priscilla and Aquila my helpers in Christ Jesus:

~KJV~

Greet Prisca and Aquila, my fellow workers in Christ Jesus,

~AMP~

May 21

Romans 16:4

Who have for my life laid down their own necks: unto whom not only I give thanks, but also all the churches of the Gentiles.

~KJV~

who risked their own necks [endangering their very lives] for my life. To them not only do I give thanks, but also all the churches of the Gentiles.

~AMP~

A New Day: A Daily Dose of Jesus Sprinkles

May 22

Psalms 22:10

I was cast upon thee from the womb: thou art my God from my mother's belly.

~KJV~

I was cast upon You from birth; From my mother's womb You have been my God.

~AMP~

May 23

Luke 2:51

And he went down with them, and came to Nazareth, and was subject unto them: but his mother kept all these sayings in her heart.

~KJV~

He went down to Nazareth with them, and was continually submissive and obedient to them; and His mother treasured all these things in her heart.

~AMP~

May 24

Genesis 30:22

And God remembered Rachel, and God hearkened to her, and opened her womb.

~KJV~

Then God remembered [the prayers of] Rachel, and God thought of her and opened her womb [so that she would conceive].

~AMP~

May 25

Genesis 30:23

And she conceived, and bare a son; and said, God hath taken away my reproach:

~KJV~

So she conceived and gave birth to a son; and she said, "God has taken away my disgrace and humiliation."

~AMP~

May 26

Genesis 30:24

And she called his name Joseph; and said, The Lord shall add to me another son.

~KJV~

She named him Joseph (may He add) and said, "May the Lord add to me another son."

~AMP~

May 27

Matthew 12:46

While he yet talked to the people, behold, his mother and his brethren stood without, desiring to speak with him.

~KJV~

While He was still talking to the crowds, it happened that His mother and brothers stood outside, asking to speak to Him.

~AMP~

May 28

Matthew 12:47

Then one said unto him, Behold, thy mother and thy brethren stand without, desiring to speak with thee.

~KJV~

Someone said to Him, "Look! Your mother and Your brothers are standing outside asking to speak to You."

~AMP~

May 29

Matthew 12:48

But he answered and said unto him that told him, Who is my mother? and who are my brethren?

~KJV~

But Jesus replied to the one who told Him, "Who is My mother and who are My brothers?"

~AMP~

May 30

Matthew 12:49

And he stretched forth his hand toward his disciples, and said, Behold my mother and my brethren!

~KJV~

And stretching out His hand toward His disciples [and all His other followers], He said, "Here are My mother and My brothers!

~AMP~

May 31

Matthews 12:50

For whosoever shall do the will of my Father which is in heaven, the same is my brother, and sister, and mother.

~KJV~

For [a]whoever does the will of My Father who is in heaven [by believing in Me, and following Me] is My brother and sister and mother."

~AMP~

A New Day: *A Daily Dose of Jesus Sprinkles*

Shunda White

June

~Inspired by Ramon Ogden~

A New Day: A Daily Dose of Jesus Sprinkles

June 1

Genesis 15:15

And thou shalt go to thy fathers in peace; thou shalt be buried in a good old age.

~KJV~

As for you, you shall [die and] go to your fathers in peace; you shall be buried at a good old age.

~AMP~

June 2

Genesis 17:4

As for me, behold, my covenant is with thee, and thou shalt be a father of many nations.

~KJV~

"As for Me, behold, My covenant is with you, And [as a result] you shall be the father of many nations.

~AMP~

June 3

Psalm 103:13

Like as a father pitieth his children, so
the Lord pitieth them that fear him.

~KJV~

Just as a father loves his children,
So the Lord loves those who fear *and* worship Him
[with awe-filled respect and deepest reverence

~AMP~

June 4

Psalm 127:3-5

Lo, children are an heritage of the Lord: and the fruit of the womb is his reward. As arrows are in the hand of a mighty man; so are children of the youth. Happy is the man that hath his quiver full of them: they shall not be ashamed, but they shall speak with the enemies in the gate.

~KJV~

Behold, children are a heritage *and* gift from the Lord, The fruit of the womb a reward.
Like arrows in the hand of a warrior, So are the children of one's youth. How blessed [happy and fortunate] is the man whose quiver is filled with them; They will not be ashamed When they speak with their enemies [in gatherings] at the [city] gate.

~AMP~

June 5

Proverbs 23:24

The father of the righteous shall greatly rejoice: and he that begetteth a wise child shall have joy of him.

~KJV~

The father of the righteous will greatly rejoice, And he who sires a wise child will have joy in him.

~AMP~

June 6

Proverbs 20:7

The just man walketh in his integrity: his children are blessed after him.

~KJV~

The righteous man who walks in integrity *and* lives life in accord with his [godly] beliefs—
How blessed [happy and spiritually secure] are his children after him [who have his example to follow].

~AMP~

June 7

Proverbs 10:1

The proverbs of Solomon. A wise son maketh a glad father: but a foolish son is the heaviness of his mother.

~KJV~

A wise son makes a father glad,
But a foolish [stubborn] son [who refuses to learn] is a grief to his mother.

~AMP~

June 8

1 Thessalonians 2:11-12

As ye know how we exhorted and comforted and charged every one of you, as a father doth his children, That ye would walk worthy of God, who hath called you unto his kingdom and glory.

~KJV~

For you know how we were exhorting and encouraging and imploring each one of you just as a father does [in dealing with] his own children, [guiding you] [12] to live lives [of honor, moral courage, and personal integrity] worthy of the God who [saves you and] calls you into His own kingdom and glory.

~AMP~

June 9

Exodus 20:12

Honour thy father and thy mother: that thy days may be long upon the land which the Lord thy God giveth thee.

~KJV~

"Honor (respect, obey, care for) your father and your mother, so that your days may be prolonged in the land the Lord your God gives you.

~AMP~

June 10

Proverbs 3:11

My son, despise not the chastening of the Lord; neither be weary of his correction:

~KJV~

My son, do not reject *or* take lightly the discipline of the Lord[learn from your mistakes and the testing that comes from His correction through discipline]; Nor despise His rebuke,

~AMP~

June 11

Proverbs 23:22

Hearken unto thy father that begat thee, and despise not thy mother when she is old.

~KJV~

Listen to your father, who sired you,
And do not despise your mother when she is old.

~AMP~

June 12

Proverbs 4:1

Hear, ye children, the instruction of a father, and attend to know understanding.

~KJV~

Hear, O children, the instruction of a father, And pay attention [and be willing to learn] so that you may gain understanding *and* intelligent discernment.

~AMP~

June 13

Proverbs 4:3-4

For I was my father's son, tender and only beloved in the sight of my mother. He taught me also, and said unto me, Let thine heart retain my words: keep my commandments, and live.

~KJV~

When I was a son with my father (David), Tender and the only son in the sight of my mother (Bathsheba), He taught me and said to me, "Let your heart hold fast my words; Keep my commandments and live.

~AMP~

June 14

Ephesians 6:4

And, ye fathers, provoke not your children to wrath: but bring them up in the nurture and admonition of the Lord.

~KJV~

Fathers, do not provoke your children to anger [do not exasperate them to the point of resentment with demands that are trivial or unreasonable or humiliating or abusive; nor by showing favoritism or indifference to any of them], but bring them up [tenderly, with lovingkindness] in the discipline and instruction of the Lord.

~AMP~

June 15

Colossians 3:21

Fathers, provoke not your children to anger, lest they be discouraged.

~KJV~

Fathers, do not provoke *or* irritate *or* exasperate your children [with demands that are trivial or unreasonable or humiliating or abusive; nor by favoritism or indifference; treat them tenderly with lovingkindness], so they will not lose heart *and* become discouraged *or* unmotivated [with their spirits broken].

~AMP~

A New Day: A Daily Dose of Jesus Sprinkles

June 16

John 3:16

For God so loved the world, that he gave his only begotten Son, that whosoever believeth in him should not perish, but have everlasting life.

~KJV~

"For God so [greatly] loved *and* dearly prized the world, that He [even] gave His [One and] only begotten Son, so that whoever believes *and* trusts in Him [as Savior] shall not perish, but have eternal life.

~AMP~

June 17

Proverbs 19:18

Chasten thy son while there is hope, and let not thy soul spare for his crying.

~KJV~

Discipline *and* teach your son while there is hope, And do not [indulge your anger or resentment by imposing inappropriate punishment nor] desire his destruction

~AMP~

June 18

Hebrew 12:7

If ye endure chastening, God dealeth with you as with sons; for what son is he whom the father chasteneth not?

~KJV~

You must submit to [correction for the purpose of] discipline; God is dealing with you as with sons; for what son is there whom his father does not discipline?

~AMP~

June 19

Matthew 7:11

If ye then, being evil, know how to give good gifts unto your children, how much more shall your Father which is in heaven give good things to them that ask him?

~KJV~

If you then, evil (sinful by nature) as you are, know how to give good *and* advantageous gifts to your children, how much more will your Father who is in heaven [perfect as He is] give what is good *and* advantageous to those who keep on asking Him.

~AMP~

A New Day: A Daily Dose of Jesus Sprinkles

June 20

Matthew 23:9

And call no man your father upon the earth: for one is your Father, which is in heaven.

~KJV~

Do not call *anyone* on earth [who guides you spiritually] your father; for One is your Father, He who is in heaven.

~AMP~

June 21

Galatians 4:6

And because ye are sons, God hath sent forth the Spirit of his Son into your hearts, crying, Abba, Father.

~KJV~

And because you [really] are [His] sons, God has sent the Spirit of His Son into our hearts, crying out, "Abba! Father!"

~AMP~

June 22

Ephesians 4:4-6

There is one body, and one Spirit, even as ye are called in one hope of your calling; One Lord, one faith, one baptism, One God and Father of all, who is above all, and through all, and in you all.

~KJV~

There is one body [of believers] and one Spirit—just as you were called to one hope when called [to salvation]— **5** one Lord, one faith, one baptism, **6** one God and Father of us all who is [sovereign] overall and [working] through all and [living] in all.

~AMP~

June 23

Joshua 1:9

Have not I commanded thee? Be strong and of a good courage; be not afraid, neither be thou dismayed: for the Lord thy God is with thee whithersoever thou goest.

~KJV~

Have I not commanded you? Be strong and courageous! Do not be terrified or dismayed (intimidated), for the Lord your God is with you wherever you go."

~AMP~

A New Day: A Daily Dose of Jesus Sprinkles

June 24

Deuteronomy 1:29-31

Then I said unto you, Dread not, neither be afraid of them. The Lord your God which goeth before you, he shall fight for you, according to all that he did for you in Egypt before your eyes; And in the wilderness, where thou hast seen how that the Lord thy God bare thee, as a man doth bear his son, in all the way that ye went, until ye came into this place.

~KJV~

Then I said to you, 'Do not be shocked, nor fear them. ³⁰ The Lord your God who goes before you will fight for you Himself, just as He did for you in Egypt before your [very] eyes, ³¹ and in the wilderness where you saw how the Lord your God carried *and* protected you, just as a man carries his son, all along the way which you traveled until you arrived at this place.'

~AMP~

June 25

1 Corinthians 13:11

When I was a child, I spake as a child, I understood as a child, I thought as a child: but when I became a man, I put away childish things.

~KJV~

When I was a child, I talked like a child, I thought like a child, I reasoned like a child; when I became a man, I did away with childish things.

~AMP~

June 26

Proverbs 22:15

Foolishness is bound in the heart of a child; but the rod of correction shall drive it far from him.

~KJV~

Foolishness is bound up in the heart of a child; The rod of discipline [correction administered with godly wisdom and lovingkindness] will remove it far from him.

~AMP~

June 27

Proverbs 23:13

Withhold not correction from the child: for if thou beatest him with the rod, he shall not die.

~KJV~

Do not withhold discipline from the child;
If you [a]swat him with a *reed-like* rod [applied with godly wisdom], he will not die.

~AMP~

June 28

Proverbs 29:3

Whoso loveth wisdom rejoiceth his father: but he that keepeth company with harlots spendeth his substance.

~KJV~

A man who loves [skillful and godly] wisdom makes his father joyful, But he who associates with prostitutes wastes his wealth.

~AMP~

June 29

Proverbs 17:21

He that begetteth a fool doeth it to his sorrow: and the father of a fool hath no joy.

~KJV~

He who becomes the parent of a fool [who is spiritually blind] does so to his sorrow,
And the father of a fool [who is spiritually blind] has no joy.

~AMP~

A New Day: *A Daily Dose of Jesus Sprinkles*

June 30

Proverbs 19:13

A foolish son is the calamity of his father: and the contentions of a wife are a continual dropping.

~KJV~

A foolish (ungodly) son is destruction to his father, And the contentions of a [quarrelsome] wife are like a constant dripping [of water].

~AMP~

Shunda White

July

~Inspired by Nijah Fields~

A New Day: A Daily Dose of Jesus Sprinkles

July 1

Genesis 4:7

If thou doest well, shalt thou not be accepted? and if thou doest not well, sin lieth at the door. And unto thee shall be his desire, and thou shalt rule over him.

~KJV~

f you do well [believing Me and doing what is acceptable and pleasing to Me], will you not be accepted? And if you do not do well [but ignore My instruction], sin crouches at your door; its desire is for you [to overpower you], but you must master it."

~AMP~

July 2

Numbers 27:3

Our father died in the wilderness, and he was not in the company of them that gathered themselves together against the Lord in the company of Korah; but died in his own sin, and had no sons.

~KJV~

"Our father died in the wilderness. He was not among those who assembled together against the Lord in the company of Korah, but he died for his own sin [as did all those who rebelled at Kadesh], and he had no sons.

~AMP~

July 3

2 Chronicles 25:4

But he slew not their children, but did as it is written in the law in the book of Moses, where the Lord commanded, saying, The fathers shall not die for the children, neither shall the children die for the fathers, but every man shall die for his own sin.

~KJV~

But he did not kill their children; for he did as it is written in the Law, in the Book of Moses, where the Lord commanded, "The fathers shall not die for the children, nor the children die for the fathers, but each shall be put to death for his own sin."

~AMP~

July 4

Psalm 19:13

Keep back thy servant also from presumptuous sins; let them not have dominion over me: then shall I be upright, and I shall be innocent from the great transgression.

~KJV~

Also keep back Your servant from presumptuous (deliberate, willful) sins; Let them not rule and have control over me. Then I will be blameless (complete), And I shall be acquitted of great transgression.

~AMP~

July 5

Psalm 32:1

Blessed is he whose transgression is forgiven,
whose sin is covered.

~KJV~

Blessed [fortunate, prosperous, favored by God] is
he whose transgression is forgiven,
And whose sin is covered.

~AMP~

July 6

Psalm 51:3

For I acknowledge my transgressions: and my sin is ever before me.

~KJV~

For I am conscious of my transgressions and I acknowledge them; My sin is always before me.

~AMP~

July 7

Proverbs 14:9

Fools make a mock at sin: but among the righteous there is favour.

~KJV~

Fools mock sin [but sin mocks the fools],
But among the upright there is good will and the favor and blessing of God

~AMP~

July 8

Proverbs 14:34

Righteousness exalteth a nation: but sin is a reproach to any people.

~KJV~

Righteousness [moral and spiritual integrity and virtuous character] exalts a nation, But sin is a disgrace to any people.

~KJV~

July 9
Psalm 51:7

Purge me with hyssop, and I shall be clean: wash me, and I shall be whiter than snow.

~KJV~

Purify me with hyssop, and I will be clean; Wash me, and I will be whiter than snow.

~AMP~

July 10

Numbers 15:28

And the priest shall make an atonement for the soul that sinneth ignorantly, when he sinneth by ignorance before the Lord, to make an atonement for him; and it shall be forgiven him.

~KJV~

The priest shall make atonement before the Lord for the person who commits an error when he sins unintentionally, making atonement for him so that he may be forgiven.

~AMP~

July 11

Psalm 57:10

For thy mercy is great unto the heavens, and thy truth unto the clouds.

~KJV~

For Your faithfulness and lovingkindness are great, reaching to the heavens, And Your truth to the clouds.

~AMP~

July 12

Matthew 12:31

Wherefore I say unto you, All manner of sin and blasphemy shall be forgiven unto men: but the blasphemy against the Holy Ghost shall not be forgiven unto men.

~KJV~

"Therefore I say to you, every sin and blasphemy [every evil, abusive, injurious speaking, or indignity against sacred things] will be forgiven people, but [a]blasphemy against the [Holy] Spirit will not be forgiven.

~AMP~

July 13

John 1:29

The next day John seeth Jesus coming unto him, and saith, Behold the Lamb of God, which taketh away the sin of the world.

~KJV~

The next day he saw Jesus coming to him and said, "Look! The Lamb of God who takes away the sin of the world!

~AMP~

July 14

John 8:7

So when they continued asking him, he lifted up himself, and said unto them, He that is without sin among you, let him first cast a stone at her.

~KJV~

However, when they persisted in questioning Him, He straightened up and said, "He who is without [any] sin among you, let him be the first to throw a stone at her."

~AMP~

July 15

Hosea 4:7

As they were increased, so they sinned against me: therefore will I change their glory into shame.

~KJV~

The more they multiplied [in numbers and increased in power], the more they sinned against Me; I will change their glory into shame.

~AMP~

A New Day: A Daily Dose of Jesus Sprinkles

July 16

John 3:16

For God so loved the world, that he gave his only begotten Son, that whosoever believeth in him should not perish, but have everlasting life.

~KJV~

"For God so [greatly] loved and dearly prized the world, that He [even] gave His [One and] only begotten Son, so that whoever believes and trusts in Him [as Savior] shall not perish, but have eternal life.

~AMP~

July 17

Romans 5:20

Moreover the law entered, that the offence might abound. But where sin abounded, grace did much more abound:

~KJV~

But the Law came to increase and expand [the awareness of] the trespass [by defining and unmasking sin]. But where sin increased, [God's remarkable, gracious gift of] grace [His unmerited favor] has surpassed it and increased all the more,

~AMP~

July 18

Romans 5:21

That as sin hath reigned unto death, even so might grace reign through righteousness unto eternal life by Jesus Christ our Lord.

~KJV~

so that, as sin reigned in death, so also grace would reign through righteousness which brings eternal life through Jesus Christ our Lord.

~AMP~

July 19

Romans 7:14

For we know that the law is spiritual: but I am carnal, sold under sin.

~KJV~

We know that the Law is spiritual, but I am a creature of the flesh [worldly, self-reliant—carnal and unspiritual], sold into slavery to sin [and serving under its control].

~AMP~

July 20

Romans 14:23

And he that doubteth is damned if he eat, because he eateth not of faith: for whatsoever is not of faith is sin.

~KJV~

But he who is uncertain [about eating a particular thing] is condemned if he eats, because he is not acting from faith. Whatever is not from faith is sin [whatever is done with doubt is sinful].

~AMP~

July 21

1 Peter 2:24

Who his own self bare our sins in his own body on the tree, that we, being dead to sins, should live unto righteousness: by whose stripes ye were healed.

~KJV~

He personally carried our sins in His body on the [a]cross [willingly offering Himself on it, as on an altar of sacrifice], so that we might die to sin [becoming immune from the penalty and power of sin] and live for righteousness; for by His wounds you [who believe] have been healed.

~AMP~

July 22

Job 10:14

If I sin, then thou markest me, and thou wilt not acquit me from mine iniquity.

~KJV~

If I sin, then You would take note and observe me, And You would not acquit me of my guilt.

~AMP~

July 23

Psalm 39:1

I said, I will take heed to my ways, that I sin not with my tongue: I will keep my mouth with a bridle, while the wicked is before me.

~KJV~

I said, "I will guard my ways That I may not sin with my tongue; I will muzzle my mouth While the wicked are in my presence."

~AMP~

July 24

Proverb 8:35

For whoso findeth me findeth life, and shall obtain favour of the Lord.

~KJV~

"For whoever finds me (Wisdom) finds life And obtains favor and grace from the Lord.

~AMP~

July 25

Ezekiel 18:4

Behold, all souls are mine; as the soul of the father, so also the soul of the son is mine: the soul that sinneth, it shall die.

~KJV~

Behold (pay close attention), all souls are Mine; the soul of the father as well as the soul of the son is Mine. The soul who sins will die.

~AMP~

July 26

John 8:11

She said, No man, Lord. And Jesus said unto her, Neither do I condemn thee: go, and sin no more.

~KJV~

She answered, "No one, Lord!" And Jesus said, "I do not condemn you either. Go. From now on sin no more."]

~AMP~

July 27

1 Corinthians 15:34

Awake to righteousness, and sin not; for some have not the knowledge of God: I speak this to your shame.

~KJV~

Be sober-minded [be sensible, wake up from your spiritual stupor] as you ought, and stop sinning; for some [of you] have no knowledge of God [you are disgracefully ignorant of Him, and ignore His truths]. I say this to your shame.

~AMP~

July 28

Ephesians 4:26

Be ye angry, and sin not: let not the sun go down upon your wrath:

~KJV~

BE ANGRY [at sin—at immorality, at injustice, at ungodly behavior], YET DO NOT SIN; do not let your anger [cause you shame, nor allow it to] last until the sun goes down.

~AMP~

July 29

Romans 3:23

For all have sinned, and come short of the glory of God;

~KJV~

since all have sinned and continually fall short of the glory of God,

~AMP~

A New Day: A Daily Dose of Jesus Sprinkles

July 30

Hosea 4:6

My people are destroyed for lack of knowledge: because thou hast rejected knowledge, I will also reject thee, that thou shalt be no priest to me: seeing thou hast forgotten the law of thy God, I will also forget thy children.

~KJV~

My people are destroyed for lack of knowledge [of My law, where I reveal My will]. Because you [the priestly nation] have rejected knowledge, I will also reject you from being My priest. Since you have forgotten the law of your God, I will also forget your children.

~AMP~

July 31

Haggai 1:7

Thus saith the Lord of hosts; Consider your ways.

~KJV~

Thus says the Lord of hosts, "Consider your ways and thoughtfully reflect on your conduct!

~AMP~

A New Day: *A Daily Dose of Jesus Sprinkles*

Shunda White

August

A New Day: *A Daily Dose of Jesus Sprinkles*

August 1

2 Corinthian 5:17

Therefore if any man be in Christ, he is a new creature: old things are passed away; behold, all things are become new.

~KJV~

Therefore if anyone is in Christ [that is, grafted in, joined to Him by faith in Him as Savior], he is a new creature [reborn and renewed by the Holy Spirit]; the old things [the previous moral and spiritual condition] have passed away. Behold, new things have come [because spiritual awakening brings a new life].

~AMP~

A New Day: *A Daily Dose of Jesus Sprinkles*

August 2

Ezekiel 11:9

And I will bring you out of the midst thereof, and deliver you into the hands of strangers, and will execute judgments among you.

~KJV~

And I will bring you out of the midst of the city and hand you over to strangers and execute judgment against you.

~AMP~

August 3

Ezekiel 18:31

Cast away from you all your transgressions, whereby ye have transgressed; and make you a new heart and a new spirit: for why will ye die, O house of Israel?

~KJV~

Cast away from you all your transgressions which you have committed [against Me], and make yourselves a new heart and a new spirit! For why should you die, O house of Israel?

~AMP~

August 4

Matthew 20:28

Even as the Son of man came not to be ministered unto, but to minister, and to give his life a ransom for many.

~KJV~

just as the Son of Man did not come to be served, but to serve, and to give His life as a ransom for many [paying the price to set them free from the penalty of sin]."

~AMP~

August 5

2 Corinthians 3:6

Who also hath made us able ministers of the new testament; not of the letter, but of the spirit: for the letter killeth, but the spirit giveth life.

~KJV~

He has qualified us [making us sufficient] as ministers of a new covenant [of salvation through Christ], not of the letter [of a written code] but of the Spirit; for the letter [of the Law] kills [by revealing sin and demanding obedience], but the Spirit gives life.

~AMP~

August 6

Ephesians 4:24

And that ye put on the new man, which after God is created in righteousness and true holiness.

~KJV~

and put on the new self [the regenerated and renewed nature], created in God's image, [godlike] in the righteousness and holiness of the truth [living in a way that expresses to God your gratitude for your salvation].

~AMP~

August 7

Ezekiel 36:25

Then will I sprinkle clean water upon you, and ye shall be clean: from all your filthiness, and from all your idols, will I cleanse you.

~KJV~

Then I will sprinkle clean water on you, and you will be clean; I will cleanse you from all your uncleanness and from all your idols.

~AMP~

A New Day: A Daily Dose of Jesus Sprinkles

August 8
Ezekiel 36:26

A new heart also will I give you, and a new spirit will I put within you: and I will take away the stony heart out of your flesh, and I will give you an heart of flesh.

~KJV~

Moreover, I will give you a new heart and put a new spirit within you, and I will remove the heart of stone from your flesh and give you a heart of flesh.

~AMP~

August 9

Ezekiel 36:27

And I will put my spirit within you, and cause you to walk in my statutes, and ye shall keep my judgments, and do them.

~KJV~

I will put my Spirit within you and cause you to walk in My statutes, and you will keep My ordinances and do them.

~AMP~

A New Day: *A Daily Dose of Jesus Sprinkles*

August 10

Ezekiel 36:28

And ye shall dwell in the land that I gave to your fathers; and ye shall be my people, and I will be your God.

~KJV~

You will live in the land that I gave to your fathers; and you will be My people, and I will be your God.

~AMP~

August 11

Colossians 3:10

And have put on the new man, which is renewed in knowledge after the image of him that created him:

~KJV

and have put on the new [spiritual] self who is being continually renewed in true knowledge in the image of Him who created the new self—

~AMP~

A New Day: *A Daily Dose of Jesus Sprinkles*

August 12

Isaiah 43:19

Behold, I will do a new thing; now it shall spring forth; shall ye not know it? I will even make a way in the wilderness, and rivers in the desert.

~KJV~

"Listen carefully, I am about to do a new thing,
Now it will spring forth;
Will you not be aware of it?
I will even put a road in the wilderness,
Rivers in the desert.
~AMP~

August 13

Psalm 51:10

Create in me a clean heart, O God; and renew a right spirit within me.

~KJV~

Create in me a clean heart, O God, And renew a right and steadfast spirit within me.

~AMP~

August 14

Isaiah 43:10

Ye are my witnesses, saith the Lord, and my servant whom I have chosen: that ye may know and believe me, and understand that I am he: before me there was no God formed, neither shall there be after me.

~KJV~

"You are My witnesses," declares the Lord, "And My servant whom I have chosen, That you may know and believe Me And understand that I am He. Before Me there was no God formed, And there will be none after Me.

~AMP~

August 15

John 13:15

For I have given you an example, that ye should do as I have done to you.

~KJV~

For I gave you [this as] an example, so that you should do [in turn] as I did to you.

~AMP~

August 16

John 3:16

For God so loved the world, that he gave his only begotten Son, that whosoever believeth in him should not perish, but have everlasting life.

~KJV~

"For God so [greatly] loved and dearly prized the world, that He [even] gave His [One and] [a]only begotten Son, so that whoever believes and trusts in Him [as Savior] shall not perish, but have eternal life.

~AMP~

August 17

Isaiah 43:2

When thou passest through the waters, I will be with thee; and through the rivers, they shall not overflow thee: when thou walkest through the fire, thou shalt not be burned; neither shall the flame kindle upon thee.

~KJV~

"When you pass through the waters, I will be with you; And through the rivers, they will not overwhelm you. When you walk through fire, you will not be scorched, Nor will the flame burn you.

~AMP~

August 18
Isaiah 43:4

Since thou wast precious in my sight, thou hast been honourable, and I have loved thee: therefore will I give men for thee, and people for thy life.
~KJV~

"Because you are precious in My sight,
You are honored and I love you,
I will give other men in return for you and other peoples in exchange for your life.
~AMP~

August 19

Lamentations 3:22

It is of the Lord's mercies that we are not consumed, because his compassions fail not.

~KJV~

It is because of the LORD'S lovingkindnesses that we are not consumed, Because His [tender] compassions never fail.

~AMP~

A New Day: A Daily Dose of Jesus Sprinkles

August 20

Lamentations 3:23

They are new every morning: great is thy faithfulness.

~KJV~

They are new every morning;
Great and beyond measure is Your faithfulness.
~AMP~

August 21

Colossians 3:14

And above all these things put on charity, which is the bond of perfectness.

~KJV~

Beyond all these things put on and wrap yourselves in [unselfish] love, which is the perfect bond of unity [for everything is bound together in agreement when each one seeks the best for others].

~AMP~

August 22

Titus 3:5

Not by works of righteousness which we have done, but according to his mercy he saved us, by the washing of regeneration, and renewing of the Holy Ghost;

~KJV~

He saved us, not because of any works of righteousness that we have done, but because of His own compassion and mercy, by the cleansing of the new birth (spiritual transformation, regeneration) and renewing by the Holy Spirit,

~AMP~

August 23

Romans 12:2

And be not conformed to this world: but be ye transformed by the renewing of your mind, that ye may prove what is that good, and acceptable, and perfect, will of God.

~KJV~

And do not be conformed to this world [any longer with its superficial values and customs], but be transformed and progressively changed [as you mature spiritually] by the renewing of your mind [focusing on godly values and ethical attitudes], so that you may prove [for yourselves] what the will of God is, that which is good and acceptable and perfect [in His plan and purpose for you].

~AMP~

August 24

Psalms 104:30

Thou sendest forth thy spirit, they are created: and thou renewest the face of the earth.

~KJV~

You send out Your Spirit, they are created; You renew the face of the ground.

~AMP~

August 25

2 Corinthians 4:17

For our light affliction, which is but for a moment, worketh for us a far more exceeding and eternal weight of glory;

~KJV~

For our momentary, light distress [this passing trouble] is producing for us an eternal weight of glory [a fullness] beyond all measure [surpassing all comparisons, a transcendent splendor and an endless blessedness]!

~AMP~

August 26

Ephesians 4:23

And be renewed in the spirit of your mind;

~KJV~

and be continually renewed in the spirit of your mind [having a fresh, untarnished mental and spiritual attitude],

~AMP~

August 27

2 Corinthians 4:16

For which cause we faint not; but though our outward man perish, yet the inward man is renewed day by day.

~KJV~

Therefore we do not become discouraged [spiritless, disappointed, or afraid]. Though our outer self is [progressively] wasting away, yet our inner self is being [progressively] renewed day by day.

~AMP~

August 28

2 Corinthians 4:18

While we look not at the things which are seen, but at the things which are not seen: for the things which are seen are temporal; but the things which are not seen are eternal.

~KJV~

So we look not at the things which are seen, but at the things which are unseen; for the things which are visible are temporal [just brief and fleeting], but the things which are invisible are everlasting and imperishable.

~AMP~

August 29

1 Corinthians 2:9

But as it is written, Eye hath not seen, nor ear heard, neither have entered into the heart of man, the things which God hath prepared for them that love him.

~KJV~

but just as it is written [in Scripture], "THINGS WHICH THE EYE HAS NOT SEEN AND THE EAR HAS NOT HEARD, AND WHICH HAVE NOT ENTERD THE HEART OF MAN, ALL THAT GOD HAS PREPARED FOR THOSE WHO LOVE HIM [who hold Him in affectionate reverence, who obey Him, and who gratefully recognize the benefits that He has bestowed]."

~AMP~

A New Day: *A Daily Dose of Jesus Sprinkles*

August 30

Isaiah 43:18

Remember ye not the former things, neither consider the things of old.

~KJV~

"Do not remember the former things,
Or ponder the things of the past.
~AMP~

August 31

Haggai 1:7

Thus saith the Lord of hosts; Consider your ways.

~KJV~

Thus says the Lord of hosts, "Consider your ways and thoughtfully reflect on your conduct!

~AMP~

A New Day: *A Daily Dose of Jesus Sprinkles*

Shunda White

September

~Inspired by Josslyn White~

A New Day: *A Daily Dose of Jesus Sprinkles*

September 1

John 8:12

Then spake Jesus again unto them, saying, I am the light of the world: he that followeth me shall not walk in darkness, but shall have the light of life.

~KJV~

Once more Jesus addressed the crowd. He said, "[a]I am the Light of the world. He who follows Me will not walk in the darkness, but will have the Light of life."

~AMP~

A New Day: *A Daily Dose of Jesus Sprinkles*

September 2

Matthew 5:17

Think not that I am come to destroy the law, or the prophets: I am not come to destroy, but to fulfil.

~KJV~

"Do not think that I came to do away with or undo the Law [of Moses] or the [writings of the] Prophets; I did not come to destroy but to fulfill.

~AMP~

September 3

Matthew 5:14

Ye are the light of the world. A city that is set on an hill cannot be hid.

~KJV~

"You are the light of [Christ to] the world. A city set on a hill cannot be hidden;

~AMP~

September 4

John 9:5

As long as I am in the world, I am the light of the world.

~KJV~

As long as I am in the world, I am the Light of the world [giving guidance through My word and works]."

~AMP~

September 5

2 Corinthians 4:4

In whom the god of this world hath blinded the minds of them which believe not, lest the light of the glorious gospel of Christ, who is the image of God, should shine unto them.

~KJV~

among them the god of this world [Satan] has blinded the minds of the unbelieving to prevent them from seeing the illuminating light of the gospel of the glory of Christ, who is the image of God.

~AMP~

September 6

Psalms 37:4

Delight thyself also in the Lord: and he shall give thee the desires of thine heart.

~KJV~

Delight yourself in the Lord, And He will give you the desires and petitions of your heart

~AMP~

September 7

1 Kings 10:9

Blessed be the Lord thy God, which delighted in thee, to set thee on the throne of Israel: because the Lord loved Israel for ever, therefore made he thee king, to do judgment and justice.

~KJV~

Blessed be the Lord your God who delighted in you to set you on the throne of Israel! Because the LORD loved Israel forever, He made you king to execute justice and righteousness."

~AMP~

September 8

Psalm 37:23

The steps of a good man are ordered by the Lord: and he delighteth in his way.

~KJV~

The steps of a [good and righteous] man are directed and established by the Lord, And He delights in his way [and blesses his path].

~AMP~

September 9

Psalm 40:8

I delight to do thy will, O my God: yea, thy law is within my heart.

~KJV~

"I delight to do Your will, O my God; Your law is within my heart."
~AMP~

September 10

Psalm 119:72

The law of thy mouth is better unto me than thousands of gold and silver.

~KJV~

The law from Your mouth is better to me
Than thousands of gold and silver pieces.
~AMP~

September 11

Proverb 3:12

For whom the Lord loveth he correcteth; even as a father the son in whom he delighteth.

~KJV~

For those whom the LORD loves He corrects, Even as a father corrects the son in whom he delights.

~AMP~

September 12

Proverb 11:1

A false balance is abomination to the Lord: but a just weight is his delight

~KJV~

A false balance and dishonest business practices are extremely offensive to the LORD, But an accurate scale is His delight.

~AMP~

September 13

Proverb 12:22

Lying lips are abomination to the Lord: but they that deal truly are his delight.

~KJV~

Lying lips are extremely disgusting to the Lord, But those who deal faithfully are His delight.

~AMP~

September 14

Proverb 15:8

The sacrifice of the wicked is an abomination to the Lord: but the prayer of the upright is his delight.

~KJV~

The sacrifice of the wicked is hateful and exceedingly offensive to the LORD, But the prayer of the upright is His delight!

~AMP~

September 15

Proverb 16:13

Righteous lips are the delight of kings; and they love him that speaketh right.

~KJV~

Righteous lips are the delight of kings,
And he who speaks right is loved.

~AMP~

A New Day: *A Daily Dose of Jesus Sprinkles*

September 16

John 3:16

For God so loved the world, that he gave his only begotten Son, that whosoever believeth in him should not perish, but have everlasting life.

~KJV~

"For God so [greatly] loved and dearly prized the world, that He [even] gave His [One and] [a]only begotten Son, so that whoever believes and trusts in Him [as Savior] shall not perish, but have eternal life.

~AMP~

September 17

Proverb 18:2

A fool hath no delight in understanding, but that his heart may discover itself.

~KJV~

A [closed-minded] fool does not delight in understanding, But only in revealing his personal opinions [unwittingly displaying his self-indulgence and his stupidity].

~AMP~

September 18

Proverb 19:10

Delight is not seemly for a fool; much less for a servant to have rule over princes.

~KJV~

Luxury is not fitting for a fool;
Much less for a slave to rule over princes.

~AMP~

September 19
Romans 7:22

For I delight in the law of God after the inward man:
~KJV~

For I joyfully delight in the law of God in my inner self [with my new nature],
~AMP~

A New Day: *A Daily Dose of Jesus Sprinkles*

September 20

Numbers 14:8

If the Lord delight in us, then he will bring us into this land, and give it us; a land which floweth with milk and honey.

~KJV~

If the Lord delights in us, then He will bring us into this land and give it to us, a land which flows with milk and honey.

~AMP~

September 21

Psalm 119:35

Make me to go in the path of thy commandments; for therein do I delight.

~KJV~

Make me walk in the path of Your commandments, For I delight in it.
~AMP~

September 22

Isaiah 54:7

For a small moment have I forsaken thee; but with great mercies will I gather thee.

~KJV~

"For a brief moment I abandoned you, But with great compassion *and* mercy I will gather you [to Myself again].

~AMP~

September 23

Joshua 1:9

Have not I commanded thee? Be strong and of a good courage; be not afraid, neither be thou dismayed: for the Lord thy God is with thee whithersoever thou goest.

~KJV~

Have I not commanded you? Be strong and courageous! Do not be terrified or dismayed (intimidated), for the Lord your God is with you wherever you go."

~AMP~

A New Day: *A Daily Dose of Jesus Sprinkles*

September 24

James 1:19

Wherefore, my beloved brethren, let every man be swift to hear, slow to speak, slow to wrath:

~KJV~

Understand this, my beloved brothers and sisters. Let everyone be quick to hear [be a careful, thoughtful listener], slow to speak [a speaker of carefully chosen words and], slow to anger [patient, reflective, forgiving];

~AMP~

September 25

2 Corinthians 4:8

We are troubled on every side, yet not distressed; we are perplexed, but not in despair;

~KJV~

We are pressured in every way [hedged in], but not crushed; perplexed [unsure of finding a way out], but not driven to despair;

~AMP~

September 26

2 Corinthians 4:9

Persecuted, but not forsaken; cast down, but not destroyed;

~KJV~

hunted down and persecuted, but not deserted [to stand alone]; struck down, but never destroyed;

~AMP~

September 27

Psalm 37:11

But the meek shall inherit the earth; and shall delight themselves in the abundance of peace.

~KJV~

But the humble will [at last] inherit the land And will delight themselves in abundant prosperity and peace.

~AMP~

September 28

Romans 3:28

Therefore we conclude that a man is justified by faith without the deeds of the law.

~KJV~

For we maintain that an individual is justified by faith distinctly apart from works of the Law [the observance of which has nothing to do with justification, that is, being declared free of the guilt of sin and made acceptable to God].

~AMP~

September 29

Psalm 119:70

Their heart is as fat as grease; but I delight in thy law.

~KJV~

Their heart is insensitive like fat [their minds are dull and brutal], But I delight in Your law.

~AMP~

September 30

Psalm 119:16

I will delight myself in thy statutes: I will not forget thy word.

~KJV~

I will delight in Your statutes; I will not forget Your word.

~AMP~

Shunda White

October

~Inspired by Josslyn White~

A New Day: *A Daily Dose of Jesus Sprinkles*

October 1

Psalm 105:15

Saying, Touch not mine anointed, and do my prophets no harm.

~KJV~

"Do not touch My anointed ones,
And do My prophets no harm."
~AMP~

October 2

Philippians 4:4

Rejoice in the Lord always: and again I say, Rejoice.

~KJV~

Rejoice in the Lord always [delight, take pleasure in Him]; again I will say, rejoice!

~AMP~

October 3

Psalm 19:14

Let the words of my mouth, and the meditation of my heart, be acceptable in thy sight, O Lord, my strength, and my redeemer.

~KJV~

Let the words of my mouth and the meditation of my heart Be acceptable *and* pleasing in Your sight, O Lord, my [firm, immovable] rock and my Redeemer.

~AMP~

A New Day: *A Daily Dose of Jesus Sprinkles*

October 4

Roman 12:14

Bless them which persecute you: bless, and curse not.

~KJV~

Bless those who persecute you [who cause you harm or hardship]; bless and do not curse [them].

~AMP~

October 5

Romans 12:21

Be not overcome of evil, but overcome evil with good.

~KJV~

Do not be overcome *and* conquered by evil, but overcome evil with good.

~AMP~

A New Day: *A Daily Dose of Jesus Sprinkles*

October 6

2 Corinthians 6:17

Wherefore come out from among them, and be ye separate, saith the Lord, and touch not the unclean thing; and I will receive you.

~KJV~

"SO COME OUT FROM AMONG UNBELIEVERS AND BE SEPARATE" says the Lord, "AND DO NOT TOUCH WHAT IS UNCLEAN; And I will graciously receive you and welcome you [with favor],

~AMP~

October 7

2 Chronicle 7:12

And the Lord appeared to Solomon by night, and said unto him, I have heard thy prayer, and have chosen this place to myself for an house of sacrifice.

~KJV~

Then the LORD appeared to Solomon by night and said to him: "I have heard your prayer and have chosen this place for Myself as a house of sacrifice.

~AMP~

October 8

1 John 2:15

Love not the world, neither the things that are in the world. If any man love the world, the love of the Father is not in him.

~KJV~

Do not love the world [of sin that opposes God and His precepts], nor the things that are in the world. If anyone loves the world, the love of the Father is not in him.

~AMP~

October 9

1 John 2:16

For all that is in the world, the lust of the flesh, and the lust of the eyes, and the pride of life, is not of the Father, but is of the world.

~KJV~

For all that is in the world—the lust and sensual craving of the flesh and the lust and longing of the eyes and the boastful pride of life [pretentious confidence in one's resources or in the stability of earthly things]—these do not come from the Father, but are from the world.

~AMP~

October 10

Proverb 15:18

A wrathful man stirreth up strife: but he that is slow to anger appeaseth strife.

~KJV~

A hot-tempered man stirs up strife, But he who is slow to anger and patient calms disputes.

~AMP~

October 11

Luke 1:37

For with God nothing shall be impossible."

~KJV~

For with God nothing [is or ever] shall be impossible."

~AMP~

October 12

Philippians 3:13

Brethren, I count not myself to have apprehended: but this one thing I do, forgetting those things which are behind, and reaching forth unto those things which are before,

~KJV~

[a]Brothers and sisters, I do not consider that I have made it my own yet; but one thing I do: forgetting what lies behind and reaching forward to what lies ahead,

~AMP~

October 13

Philippians 3:14

I press toward the mark for the prize of the high calling of God in Christ Jesus.

~KJV~

I press on toward the goal to win the [heavenly] prize of the upward call of God in Christ Jesus.

~AMP~

October 14

Proverb 24:19

Fret not thyself because of evil men, neither be thou envious at the wicked:

~KJV~

Do not get upset because of evildoers,
Or be envious of the wicked,

~AMP~

October 15

Ephesians 6:11

Put on the whole armour of God, that ye may be able to stand against the wiles of the devil.

~KJV~

Put on the full armor of God [for His precepts are like the splendid armor of a heavily-armed soldier], so that you may be able to [successfully] stand up against all the schemes and the strategies and the deceits of the devil.

~AMP~

A New Day: A Daily Dose of Jesus Sprinkles

October 16

John 3:16

For God so loved the world, that he gave his only begotten Son, that whosoever believeth in him should not perish, but have everlasting life.

~KJV~

"For God so [greatly] loved and dearly prized the world, that He [even] gave His [One and] [a]only begotten Son, so that whoever believes and trusts in Him [as Savior] shall not perish, but have eternal life.

~AMP~

October 17

Proverbs 17:17

A friend loveth at all times, and a brother is born for adversity.

~KJV~

A friend loves at all times, And a brother is born for adversity.

~AMP~

October 18

2 Corinthians 5:17

Therefore if any man be in Christ, he is a new creature: old things are passed away; behold, all things are become new.

~KJV~

Therefore if anyone is in Christ [that is, grafted in, joined to Him by faith in Him as Savior], he is a new creature [reborn and renewed by the Holy Spirit]; the old things [the previous moral and spiritual condition] have passed away. Behold, new things have come [because spiritual awakening brings a new life].

~AMP~

October 19

Psalm 121:1

will lift up mine eyes unto the hills, from whence cometh my help.

~KJV~

I will lift up my eyes to the hills [of Jerusalem]—
From where shall my help come?

~AMP~

October 20

Psalm 7:10

My defence is of God, which saveth the upright in heart.

~KJV~

My shield and my defense depend on God, Who saves the upright in heart.

~AMP~

October 21

Psalm 9:10

And they that know thy name will put their trust in thee: for thou, Lord, hast not forsaken them that seek thee.

~KJV~

And those who know Your name [who have experienced Your precious mercy] will put their confident trust in You, For You, O LORD, have not abandoned those who seek You.

~AMP~

October 22

Psalm 11:1

In the Lord put I my trust: how say ye to my soul, Flee as a bird to your mountain?

~KJV~

In the Lord I take refuge [and put my trust]; How can you say to me, "Flee like a bird to your mountain;

~AMP~

October 23

Psalm 18:2

The Lord is my rock, and my fortress, and my deliverer; my God, my strength, in whom I will trust; my buckler, and the horn of my salvation, and my high tower.

~KJV~

The Lord is my rock, my fortress, and the One who rescues me; My God, my rock and strength in whom I trust and take refuge; My shield, and the horn of my salvation, my high tower—my stronghold.

~AMP~

A New Day: *A Daily Dose of Jesus Sprinkles*

October 24

Psalm 121:2

My help cometh from the Lord, which made heaven and earth.

~KJV~

My help comes from the LORD, Who made heaven and earth.

~AMP~

October 25

Psalm 22:8

He trusted on the Lord that he would deliver him: let him deliver him, seeing he delighted in him.

~KJV~

"He trusted and committed himself to the LORD, let Him save him. Let Him rescue him, because He delights in him."

~AMP~

A New Day: *A Daily Dose of Jesus Sprinkles*

October 26

Psalm 26:1

Judge me, O Lord; for I have walked in mine integrity: I have trusted also in the Lord; therefore I shall not slide.

~KJV~

Vindicate me, O Lord, for I have walked in my integrity; I have [relied on and] trusted [confidently] in the LORD without wavering and I shall not slip.

~AMP~

October 27

Proverb 10:9

He that walketh uprightly walketh surely: but he that perverteth his ways shall be known.

~KJV~

He who walks in integrity and with moral character walks securely, But he who takes a crooked way will be discovered and punished.

~AMP~

October 28

Psalm 7:8

The Lord shall judge the people: judge me, O Lord, according to my righteousness, and according to mine integrity that is in me.

~KJV~

The LORD judges the peoples; Judge me, O LORD, and grant me justice according to my righteousness and according to the integrity within me.

~AMP~

October 29

Philippians 4:8

Finally, brethren, whatsoever things are true, whatsoever things are honest, whatsoever things are just, whatsoever things are pure, whatsoever things are lovely, whatsoever things are of good report; if there be any virtue, and if there be any praise, think on these things.

~KJV~

Finally, believers, whatever is true, whatever is honorable and worthy of respect, whatever is right and confirmed by God's word, whatever is pure and wholesome, whatever is lovely and brings peace, whatever is admirable and of good repute; if there is any excellence, if there is anything worthy of praise, think continually on these things [center your mind on them, and implant them in your heart].

~AMP~

October 30

Mark 14:38

Watch ye and pray, lest ye enter into temptation. The spirit truly is ready, but the flesh is weak.

~KJV~

Keep [actively] watching and praying so that you do not come into temptation; the spirit is willing, but the body is weak."

~AMP~

October 31

Genesis 50:20

But as for you, ye thought evil against me; but God meant it unto good, to bring to pass, as it is this day, to save much people alive.

~KJV~

As for you, you meant evil against me, but God meant it for good in order to bring about this present outcome, that many people would be kept alive [as they are this day].

~AMP~

A New Day: A Daily Dose of Jesus Sprinkles

November

Shunda White

A New Day: *A Daily Dose of Jesus Sprinkles*

November 1

Genesis 8:22

While the earth remaineth, seedtime and harvest, and cold and heat, and summer and winter, and day and night shall not cease.

~KJV~

"While the earth remains, Seedtime and harvest, Cold and heat, Winter and summer, And day and night Shall not cease."

~AMP~

November 2

Isaiah 55:10

For as the rain cometh down, and the snow from heaven, and returneth not thither, but watereth the earth, and maketh it bring forth and bud, that it may give seed to the sower, and bread to the eater:

~KJV~

"For as the rain and snow come down from heaven, And do not return there without watering the earth, Making it bear and sprout, And providing seed to the sower and bread to the eater,

~AMP~

November 3

1 Thessalonians 4:12

That ye may walk honestly toward them that are without, and that ye may have lack of nothing.

~KJV~

so that you will behave properly toward outsiders [exhibiting good character, personal integrity, and moral courage worthy of the respect of the outside world], and be dependent on no one and in need of nothing [be self-supporting].

~AMP~

November 4

John 4:35

Say not ye, There are yet four months, and then cometh harvest? behold, I say unto you, Lift up your eyes, and look on the fields; for they are white already to harvest.

~KJV~

Do you not say, 'It is still four months until the harvest comes?' Look, I say to you, raise your eyes and look at the fields and see, they are white for harvest.

~AMP~

November 5

Ephesians 4:16

From whom the whole body fitly joined together and compacted by that which every joint supplieth, according to the effectual working in the measure of every part, maketh increase of the body unto the edifying of itself in love.

~KJV~

From Him the whole body [the church, in all its various parts], joined and knitted firmly together by what every joint supplies, when each part is working properly, causes the body to grow and mature, building itself up in [unselfish] love.

~AMP~

November 6

1 Corinthians 3:6

I have planted, Apollos watered; but God gave the increase.

~KJV~

I planted, Apollos watered, but God [all the while] was causing the growth.

~AMP~

November 7

1 Corinthians 3:8

Now he that planteth and he that watereth are one: and every man shall receive his own reward according to his own labour.

~KJV~

He who plants and he who waters are one [in importance and esteem, working toward the same purpose]; but each will receive his own reward according to his own labor.

~AMP~

A New Day: A Daily Dose of Jesus Sprinkles

November 8

Mark 11:23

For verily I say unto you, That whosoever shall say unto this mountain, Be thou removed, and be thou cast into the sea; and shall not doubt in his heart, but shall believe that those things which he saith shall come to pass; he shall have whatsoever he saith.

~KJV~

I assure you and most solemnly say to you, whoever says to this mountain, 'Be lifted up and thrown into the sea!' and [a]does not doubt in his heart [in God's unlimited power], but believes that what he says is going to take place, it will be done for him [in accordance with God's will].

~AMP~

November 9

Mark 11:24

Therefore I say unto you, What things soever ye desire, when ye pray, believe that ye receive them, and ye shall have them.

~KJV~

For this reason I am telling you, whatever things you ask for in prayer [in accordance with God's will], believe [with confident trust] that you have received them, and they will be given to you.

~AMP~

November 10

2 Corinthians 9:10

Now he that ministereth seed to the sower both minister bread for your food, and multiply your seed sown, and increase the fruits of your righteousness;)

~KJV~

Now He who provides seed for the sower and bread for food will provide and multiply your seed for sowing [that is, your resources] and increase the harvest of your righteousness [which shows itself in active goodness, kindness, and love].

~AMP~

November 11

2 Corinthians 9:11

Being enriched in every thing to all bountifulness, which causeth through us thanksgiving to God.

~KJV~

You will be enriched in every way so that you may be generous, and this [generosity, administered] through us is producing thanksgiving to God [from those who benefit].

~AMP~

November 12

2 Thessalonian 3:12

Now them that are such we command and exhort by our Lord Jesus Christ, that with quietness they work, and eat their own bread.

~KJV~

Now such people we command and exhort in the Lord Jesus Christ to settle down and work quietly and earn their own food and other necessities [supporting themselves instead of depending on the hospitality of others].

~AMP~

November 13

Habakkuk 3:19

The Lord God is my strength, and he will make my feet like hinds' feet, and he will make me to walk upon mine high places. To the chief singer on my stringed instruments.
~KJV~

The Lord GOD is my strength [my source of courage, my invincible army]; He has made my feet [steady and sure] like hinds' feet And makes me walk [forward with spiritual confidence] on my high places [of challenge and responsibility]. For the choir director, on my stringed instruments.
~AMP~

A New Day: *A Daily Dose of Jesus Sprinkles*

November 14

1 Kings 17:16

And the barrel of meal wasted not, neither did the cruse of oil fail, according to the word of the Lord, which he spake by Elijah.

~KJV~

The bowl of flour was not exhausted nor did the jar of oil become empty, in accordance the word of the Lord which He spoke through Elijah.

~AMP~

November 15

Psalm 67:6

Then shall the earth yield her increase; and God, even our own God, shall bless us.

~KJV~

The earth has yielded its harvest [as evidence of His approval]; God, our God, blesses us.

~AMP~

A New Day: A Daily Dose of Jesus Sprinkles

November 16

John 3:16

For God so loved the world, that he gave his only begotten Son, that whosoever believeth in him should not perish, but have everlasting life.

~KJV~

"For God so [greatly] loved and dearly prized the world, that He [even] gave His [One and] [a]only begotten Son, so that whoever believes and trusts in Him [as Savior] shall not perish, but have eternal life.

~AMP~

November 17

Psalm 85:12

Yea, the Lord shall give that which is good; and our land shall yield her increase.

~KJV~

Indeed, the LORD will give what is good, And our land will yield its produce.

~AMP~

A New Day: *A Daily Dose of Jesus Sprinkles*

November 18

Jeremiah 5:24

Neither say they in their heart, Let us now fear the Lord our God, that giveth rain, both the former and the latter, in his season: he reserveth unto us the appointed weeks of the harvest.

~KJV~

'They do not say in their heart, "Let us now fear and worship the LORD our God [with profound awe and reverence], Who gives rain in its season, Both the autumn and the spring rain, Who keeps for us The appointed weeks of the harvest."

~AMP~

November 19

Colossians 2:19

And not holding the Head, from which all the body by joints and bands having nourishment ministered, and knit together, increaseth with the increase of God.

~KJV~

and not holding fast to the head [of the body, Jesus Christ], from whom the entire body, supplied and knit together by its joints and ligaments, grows with the growth [that can come only] from God.

~AMP~

November 20

2 Chronicles 20:20

And they rose early in the morning, and went forth into the wilderness of Tekoa: and as they went forth, Jehoshaphat stood and said, Hear me, O Judah, and ye inhabitants of Jerusalem; Believe in the Lord your God, so shall ye be established; believe his prophets, so shall ye prosper.

~KJV~

So they got up early in the morning and went out into the Wilderness of Tekoa; and as they went out, Jehoshaphat stood and said, "Hear me, O Judah, and you inhabitants of Jerusalem! Believe and trust in the Lord your God and you will be established (secure). Believe and trust in His prophets and succeed."

~AMP~

November 21

I Chronicle 22:11

Now, my son, the Lord be with thee; and prosper thou, and build the house of the Lord thy God, as he hath said of thee.

~KJV~

Now, my son, may the LORD be with you so that you may be successful and build the house of the LORD your God, just as He has spoken concerning you.

~AMP~

November 22

1 Chronicle 22:13

Then shalt thou prosper, if thou takest heed to fulfil the statutes and judgments which the Lord charged Moses with concerning Israel: be strong, and of good courage; dread not, nor be dismayed.

~KJV~

Then you will prosper, if you are careful to observe and fulfill the statutes and ordinances which the LORD commanded Moses concerning Israel. Be strong and courageous, do not fear nor be dismayed.

~AMP~

November 23

Galatians 6:9

And let us not be weary in well doing: for in due season we shall reap, if we faint not.

~KJV~

Let us not grow weary or become discouraged in doing good, for at the proper time we will reap, if we do not give in.

~AMP~

A New Day: *A Daily Dose of Jesus Sprinkles*

November 24

Matthew 13:30

Let both grow together until the harvest: and in the time of harvest I will say to the reapers, Gather ye together first the tares, and bind them in bundles to burn them: but gather the wheat into my barn.

~KJV~

Let them grow together until the harvest; and at harvest time I will tell the reapers, "First gather the weeds and tie them in bundles to be burned; but gather the wheat into my barn.""

~AMP~

November 25

Isaiah 9:3

Thou hast multiplied the nation, and not increased the joy: they joy before thee according to the joy in harvest, and as men rejoice when they divide the spoil.

~KJV~

You [O God] will increase the nation, You will multiply their joy; They will rejoice before You Like the joy and jubilation of the harvest, As men rejoice when they divide the spoil [of victory].

~AMP~

A New Day: A Daily Dose of Jesus Sprinkles

November 26

Proverbs 10:5

He that gathereth in summer is a wise son: but he that sleepeth in harvest is a son that causeth shame.

~KJV~

He who gathers during summer and takes advantage of his opportunities is a son who acts wisely, But he who sleeps during harvest and ignores the moment of opportunity is a son who acts shamefully.

~AMP~

November 27

Matthews 9:37

Then saith he unto his disciples, The harvest truly is plenteous, but the labourers are few;

~KJV~

Then He said to His disciples, "The harvest is [indeed] plentiful, but the workers are few.

~AMP~

A New Day: *A Daily Dose of Jesus Sprinkles*

November 28

Matthew 9:38

Pray ye therefore the Lord of the harvest, that he will send forth labourers into his harvest.

~KJV~

So pray to the Lord of the harvest to send out workers into His harvest."

~AMP~

November 29

Psalm 26:5

I have hated the congregation of evil doers; and will not sit with the wicked.

~KJV~

I hate the company of evildoers, And will not sit with the wicked.

~AMP~

November 30

Haggai 1:9

Ye looked for much, and, lo it came to little; and when ye brought it home, I did blow upon it. Why? saith the Lord of hosts. Because of mine house that is waste, and ye run every man unto his own house.

~KJV~

9 You look for much [harvest], but it comes to little; and even when you bring that home, I blow it away. Why?" says the Lord of hosts. "Because of My house, which lies in ruins while each of you runs to his own house [eager to enjoy it].

~AMP~

Shunda White

December

~Inspired by Dorjena Williams~

A New Day: *A Daily Dose of Jesus Sprinkles*

December 1

Psalm 26:5

"I have hated the congregation of evil doers; and will not sit with the wicked."

~KJV~

"I hate the company of evildoers, And will not sit with the wicked."

~AMP~

December 2

Nahum 1:7

"The Lord is good, a strong hold in the day of trouble; and he knoweth them that trust in him."

~KJV~

"The LORD is good, A strength and stronghold in the day of trouble; He knows He recognizes, cares for, and understands fully those who take refuge and trust in Him."

~AMP~

December 3

Isaiah 50:10

"Who is among you that feareth the Lord, that obeyeth the voice of his servant, that walketh in darkness, and hath no light? let him trust in the name of the Lord, and stay upon his God."

~KJV~

"Who is among you who fears the LORD, Who obeys the voice of His Servant, Yet who walks in darkness and has no light? Let him trust and be confident in the name of the LORD and let him rely on his God."

~AMP~

A New Day: *A Daily Dose of Jesus Sprinkles*

December 4

Psalm 118:8

"It is better to trust in the Lord than to put confidence in man."

~KJV~

"It is better to take refuge in the LORD Than to trust in man."

~AMP~

December 5

Psalm 22:8

"He trusted on the Lord that he would deliver him: let him deliver him, seeing he delighted in him."

~KJV~

"He trusted and committed himself to the LORD, let Him save him. Let Him rescue him, because He delights in him."

~AMP~

A New Day: A Daily Dose of Jesus Sprinkles

December 6

Psalm 143:8

"Cause me to hear thy lovingkindness in the morning; for in thee do I trust: cause me to know the way wherein I should walk; for I lift up my soul unto thee."

~KJV~

"Let me hear Your lovingkindness in the morning, For I trust in You. Teach me the way in which I should walk, For I lift up my soul to You."

~AMP~

December 7

Joshua 1:9

"Have not I commanded thee? Be strong and of a good courage; be not afraid, neither be thou dismayed: for the Lord thy God is with thee whithersoever thou goest."

~KJV~

"Have I not commanded you? Be strong and courageous! Do not be terrified or dismayed intimidated, for the LORD your God is with you wherever you go."

~AMP~

A New Day: *A Daily Dose of Jesus Sprinkles*

December 8

Psalm 9:10

"And they that know thy name will put their trust in thee: for thou, Lord, hast not forsaken them that seek thee."

~KJV~

"And those who know Your name who have experienced Your precious mercy will put their confident trust in You, For You, O LORD, have not abandoned those who seek You."

~AMP~

December 9

Proverbs 11:3

"The integrity of the upright shall guide them: but the perverseness of transgressors shall destroy them."

~KJV~

"The integrity and moral courage of the upright will guide them, But the crookedness of the treacherous will destroy them."

~KJV~

December 10

Proverbs 28:2

"He that trusteth in his own heart is a fool: but whoso walketh wisely, he shall be delivered."

~KJV~

"He who trusts confidently in his own heart is a dull, thickheaded fool, But he who walks in skillful and godly wisdom will be rescued."

~AMP~

December 11

Isaiah 43:1

"But now thus saith the Lord that created thee, O Jacob, and he that formed thee, O Israel, Fear not: for I have redeemed thee, I have called thee by thy name; thou art mine."

~KJV~

"But now, this is what the LORD, your Creator says, O Jacob, And He who formed you, O Israel, "Do not fear, for I have redeemed you [from captivity]; I have called you by name; you are Mine!"

~AMP~

December 12

Romans 15:13

"Now the God of hope fill you with all joy and peace in believing, that ye may abound in hope, through the power of the Holy Ghost."

~KJV~

May the God of hope fill you with all joy and peace in believing [through the experience of your faith] that by the power of the Holy Spirit you will abound in hope and overflow with confidence in His promises."

~AMP~

December 13

Revelation 21:5

"And he that sat upon the throne said, Behold, I make all things new. And he said unto me, Write: for these words are true and faithful."

~KJV~

"And He who sits on the throne said, "Behold, I am making all things new." Also He said, "Write, for these words are faithful and true [they are accurate, incorruptible, and trustworthy]."

~AMP~

December 14

Jeremiah 7:8

"Behold, ye trust in lying words, that cannot profit."

~KJV~

"Behold, you are trusting in deceptive and useless words that bring no benefit."

~AMP~

December 15

Proverb 11:28

"He that trusteth in his riches shall fall; but the righteous shall flourish as a branch."

~KJV~

"He who leans on and trusts in and is confident in his riches will fall, But the righteous who trust in God's provision will flourish like a green leaf."

~AMP~

December 16

Proverbs 3:5-6

5. "Trust in the Lord with all thine heart; and lean not unto thine own understanding." 6. "In all thy ways acknowledge him, and he shall direct thy paths."

~KJV~

5. "Trust in and rely confidently on the LORD with all your heart And do not rely on your own insight or understanding." 6. "In all your ways know and acknowledge and recognize Him, And He will make your paths straight and smooth [removing obstacles that block your way]."

~AMP~

December 17

Psalm 13:5

"But I have trusted in thy mercy; my heart shall rejoice in thy salvation."

~KJV~

"But I have trusted and relied on and been confident in Your lovingkindness and faithfulness; My heart shall rejoice and delight in Your salvation."

~AMP~

December 18

Proverb 6:20

"My son, keep thy father's commandment, and forsake not the law of thy mother:"

~KJV~

"My son, be guided by your father's [God-given] commandment (instruction) And do not reject the teaching of your mother;"

~AMP~

December 19

Deuteronomy 28:1

And it shall come to pass, if thou shalt hearken diligently unto the voice of the Lord thy God, to observe and to do all his commandments which I command thee this day, that the Lord thy God will set thee on high above all nations of the earth:"

~KJV~

"Now it shall be, if you diligently listen to and obey the voice of the LORD your God, being careful to do all of His commandments which I am commanding you today, the LORD your God will set you high above all the nations of the earth."

~AMP~

A New Day: *A Daily Dose of Jesus Sprinkles*

December 20

Proverbs 10:17

"He is in the way of life that keepeth instruction: but he that refuseth reproof erreth."

~KJV~

"He who learns from instruction and correction is on the [right] path of life [and for others his example is a path toward wisdom and blessing,] But he who ignores and refuses correction goes off course [and for others his example is a path toward sin and ruin]."

~AMP~

December 21

James 1:22

"But be ye doers of the word, and not hearers only, deceiving your own selves."

~KJV~

"But prove yourselves doers of the word [actively and continually obeying God's precepts,] and not merely listeners [who hear the word but fail to internalize its meaning,] deluding yourselves [by unsound reasoning contrary to the truth.]"

~AMP~

A New Day: A Daily Dose of Jesus Sprinkles

December 22

John 15:16

"Ye have not chosen me, but I have chosen you, and ordained you, that ye should go and bring forth fruit, and that your fruit should remain: that whatsoever ye shall ask of the Father in my name, he may give it you."

~KJV~

"You have not chosen Me, but I have chosen you and I have appointed and placed and purposefully planted you, so that you would go and bear fruit and keep on bearing, and that your fruit will remain and be lasting, so that whatever you ask of the Father in My name [as My representative] He may give to you."

~AMP~

December 23

Luke 6:27-28

27. "But I say unto you which hear, Love your enemies, do good to them which hate you" 28. "Bless them that curse you, and pray for them which despitefully use you."

~KJV~

27. "But I say to you who hear [Me and pay attention to My words:] Love [that is, unselfishly seek the best or higher good for] your enemies, [make it a practice to] do good to those who hate you," 28. "bless and show kindness to those who curse you, pray for those who mistreat you."

~AMP~

December 24

Romans 5:19

"For as by one man's disobedience many were made sinners, so by the obedience of one shall many be made righteous."

~KJV~

"For just as through one man's disobedience [his failure to hear, his carelessness] the many were made sinners, so through the obedience of the one Man the many will be made righteous and acceptable to God and brought into right standing with Him."

~AMP~

December 25

Romans 12:11

"Not slothful in business; fervent in spirit; serving the Lord;"

~KJV~

"never lagging behind in diligence; aglow in the Spirit, enthusiastically serving the Lord;"

~AMP~

December 26

Romans 15:32

"That I may come unto you with joy by the will of God, and may with you be refreshed."

~KJV~

"so that by God's will I may come to you with joy and find rest in your company."

~AMP~

December 27

Deuteronomy 5:33

"Ye shall walk in all the ways which the Lord your God hath commanded you, that ye may live, and that it may be well with you, and that ye may prolong your days in the land which ye shall possess."

~KJV~

"You shall walk [that is, live each and every day] in all the ways which the LORD your God has commanded you, so that you may live and so that it may be well with you, and that you may live long in the land which you will possess."

~AMP~

A New Day: *A Daily Dose of Jesus Sprinkles*

December 28

Job 8:7

"Though thy beginning was small, yet thy latter end should greatly increase."

~KJV~

"Though your beginning was insignificant, Yet your end will greatly increase."

~AMP~

December 29

Lamentation 3:22

"It is of the Lord's mercies that we are not consumed, because his compassions fail not."

~KJV~

"It is because of the LORD'S lovingkindnesses that we are not consumed, Because His [tender] compassions never fail."

~AMP~

A New Day: *A Daily Dose of Jesus Sprinkles*

December 30

Isaiah 43:18-19

18. "Remember ye not the former things, neither consider the things of old." 19. "Behold, I will do a new thing; now it shall spring forth; shall ye not know it? I will even make a way in the wilderness, and rivers in the desert."

~KJV~

18. "Do not remember the former things, Or ponder the things of the past." 19. "Listen carefully, I am about to do a new thing, Now it will spring forth; Will you not be aware of it? I will even put a road in the wilderness, Rivers in the desert."

~AMP~

December 31

Proverbs 30:6

"Add thou not unto his words, lest her reprove thee, and thou be found a liar."

~KJV~

Do not add to His words,
Or He will reprove you, and you will be found a liar.

~AMP~

A New Day: *A Daily Dose of Jesus Sprinkles*

400

www.ingramcontent.com/pod-product-compliance
Lightning Source LLC
Chambersburg PA
CBHW051358070526
44584CB00023B/3212